STAY SEXY &
DON'T GET MURDERED

THE DEFINITIVE HOW-TO GUIDE

STAY SEXY &
DON'T GET MURDERED

THE DEFINITIVE HOW-TO GUIDE

Karen Kilgariff &
Georgia Hardstark

First published in 2019 by Trapeze,
This paperback edition published in 2021 by Trapeze
an imprint of The Orion Publishing Group Ltd
Carmelite House, 50 Victoria Embankment,
London EC4Y 0DZ

An Hachette UK company

1 3 5 7 9 10 8 6 4 2

Designed by Devan Norman

Illustration credits: page 15 © Megan Lara; page 25 © Danielle Winstanley;
page 63 © Haley D. Fischer; page 95 © Rachel Ross; page 123 © Rita Garza of
RitaWorks Art & Illustration; page 153 © Jenna Beddick; page 193 © Claire
Mabbett; page 219 © Abigail Ervin; page 251 © Lucie Rice Illustration & Design;
page 285 © Lauren Goldberg
Photograph credits: page 23 © Alexandra Lucas; pages 35, 83, 119, 177, 192,
236, 258 © Leah Montagnino; pages 53, 203 © Jean Cleary; pages 58, 148 ©
Laura Kilgariff; page 90 © Lindsay Dillon; page 101 © Paul F. Tompkins; page 235
© James Kavin Cook; page 245 © MGM / Photography; page 259, 266
© Martin Hardstark. All other photos courtesy of the authors.

A CIP catalogue record for this book is
available from the British Library.

ISBN (Paperback): 978 1 398 70033 8

Printed and bound in Great Britain by Clays Ltd, Elcograf, S.p.A.

www.orionbooks.co.uk

KAREN

For Norah Grace

GEORGIA

In memory of Kim Murphy Friedman,
who therapized me through the writing of this book.

This book is dedicated to all the Murderinos out there.

We wouldn't be here if it weren't for you.

Thank you.

The names of some persons described in this book have been changed.

CONTENTS

STAY SEXY &
DON'T GET MURDERED

THE DEFINITIVE HOW-TO GUIDE

art by Megan Lara

LET'S SIT CROOKED & TALK STRAIGHT: KAREN'S INTRODUCTION

Oh, hiiiiieee!

Welcome to our first-ever book! We're so glad you could join us. Isn't it weird? We know! It is for us, too. We've never written a book before. We don't know where to put our hands!

Let us begin by saying thank you so much from the bottom of our hearts for buying this book. Your support truly means the world to us. We know some of you are young and hungry, living off of your wits and whatever spare change you can find in an old coat pocket. So this purchase was a true sacrifice. God bless you, child. The kingdom of heaven shall be yours. On the other hand, maybe you didn't buy it. Maybe you checked it out of the library and the only sacrifice you made was hauling your ass to the building. Still, we like your style. And we love libraries. Never change. There's also a chance you stole this book off your sister's nightstand while she was in the shower and then later, when she asked you if you'd seen it anywhere, immediately started a fight to throw her off your scent. Hell yeah. We support you in any way you want to support us. Bless us all, but mostly the people who actually spent money.

Wait, hold on. Maybe you're just standing in the bookstore right now skimming this introduction to assess whether or not you'll like the rest of the book. What's up, judgy? Are you pleased? Are you ever? You know what, how about you quit getting your finger grease all over our beautiful, pristine publication and just buy it. In fact, buy three. That's right. You do what we say now. Look how the tables have turned. Also, thank you! We love the push-pull of your withholding personality. It's not tiresome at all. Our overall point here is, no matter what you did to get this thing into your dirty little mitts, we appreciate your efforts.

Normally, we'd be talking to you through our podcast, where it's all microphones and couches and air. But now we've gotten paper and ink involved and things have become rather highbrow. That's right, this scrappy little true crime–comedy podcast that you've been sneak-listening to at your temp job has somehow figured out a way to transition itself into the world of . . . (SPINNING IN A CIRCLE AS ORCHESTRAL MUSIC SWELLS) . . . *literature.* We have gone from living inside your headphones to pouring ourselves out onto the page like a couple of Edna St. Vincent Millays. We invite you to drink deeply of us. We'll get you good and fucked up.

Oh, you've never heard of us before? Sure, we understand. Podcasting is a relatively new thing. Let us introduce ourselves. We are the hosts of *My*—what's that, you say? You've never listened to a podcast before and you're not sure how they work and you don't feel like getting involved? Gotcha. You're not alone. But before you run off and buy some other book with "sexy" in the title, let us tell you a little story. It's about two gals who were living passably fine lives in Los Angeles in the late 2010s. One was named Georgia, and she—to oversimplify both of their incredibly complex and varied careers—

was a Cooking Channel host, and Karen, the other one, was a sitcom writer. So, one Halloween, they're at a party together and they start chatting about a then new HBO series called *The Staircase,* which tells the story of a man going to trial for the murder of his wife. They realize they're both obsessed and are thrilled to have found someone else to talk to about it. So they do. They talk and talk. Some people join in, some dip back out, and soon the kitchen's clear of everyone except the two women. So they decide to meet for lunch. And they talk even more. Hours and hours of coffee and talking. The next time they see each other, Georgia suggests they start a true-crime podcast. Why not? They both already had podcasts of their own. They knew what it would entail. So they agreed to give it a try. CUT TO: hundreds of episodes, millions of listeners, sold-out international tour dates, and a book deal. It's kind of a feel-good story. It feels really good to us, anyway.

OK, now that we've caught everyone up, let's get back to the part about the book. We put a lot of effort into its creation, and for it, we have suffered mightily. For the past year and a half, we have been travelers set adrift on foreign seas aboard the HMS *Write-a-Book.* We set out impetuously, blindly, unfamiliar with the charted course, unsure what the food at the buffet would be like, afraid the other passengers wouldn't be nice to us. We were anxious. We were seasick. We told ourselves, "Let's just try to get through this metaphorical book boat journey in one piece. Be cool. Act natural. No, don't whistle, stupid! That's the opposite of natural. Why does everyone think whistling indicates relaxation? It's literally one of the weirdest things you can do in public without breaking the law. Blowing spurts of air out of your pursed lips to produce a raspy little song like some sad bird impersonator. No discernable tune, no clear plan. Just kind of a long, vocalized exhale through big kissy lips. What better way to let the world know you're at ease." Whoops, sorry. We got carried away there.

BECAUSE THAT, DEAR FRIENDS, IS THE POWER OF LITER-
ATURE.

Here's the bottom line—and not a lot of authors will be brave enough
to speak their truth this way, but we're just gonna say it: writing a
book is a tiny bit terrifying. It threatens to expose you as the fraud
that you are, but instead of running and hiding from the shame of it,
you just have to keep staring into the mirror. It's incredibly unnatural. You start out with an idea you like. You write that idea down.
You let it sit for five days, and when you come back to it, the words
have rearranged themselves on the page. Now it's shape-shifted into
the dumbest idea you've ever seen. So you try to fix it. And you just
keep fixing it until you go computer-blind, all the joy is drained from
your soul, and you no longer know what words mean. Then it's on to
chapter 2!

But look and listen: we did it! We actually finished a book. We
must've, right? You're holding it with your greasy fingers right now.
And we're all the better for it. Plus, now we'll finally be in the Library
of Congress! That's been on our bucket list since, like, day one.

When we first agreed to write this book, we had a lot of different
ideas about the kind of book we wanted it to be, but they all boiled
down to the same general concept: big glossy pages with pretty pictures
and a meaningful sentence or two here and there about unity or, like,
the soul. A sort of printed-up Instagram or, like, a cookbook without
all those cumbersome recipes. Short and sweet; the length and depth
of a picture book made for a gifted toddler. And then, at the very end,
maybe we'd have some kind of pull-out calendar featuring all of your
favorite true-crime authors with their shirts off. But tasteful. Basically,
we were imagining the kind of book you find in the sale bin at Urban
Outfitters a week after Christmas. In hindsight, we can admit that we
were aiming low.

But it turned out that the powers that be were expecting us to dig much deeper than that. They wanted us to give of ourselves fully. And not to use so many pictures. It was truly horrifying news.

"Just write about all the things you talk about on your show," they said. "Write what you know."

And this was the problem. You see, if there's anything we've learned in our three years of doing this podcast, it's that we don't know anything. At all. We don't know about geography or pronunciations or Roman numerals or percentages or the Cherry Hill Mall in New Jersey or dates or names or the law or really anything at all. It's been a very humbling experience. And also a hilarious one. Being so consistently wrong made us very self-conscious about our lack of education and our habits of assumption and unabashedly filling in blanks. Every time we record, we know there's a trapdoor of ignorance waiting beneath our feet. It's made us a little skittish and untrusting of the floor. And in the beginning, it made us feel like we were doing it wrong.

But here's the irony (*a literary term*): people still listened. Some even loved it. Our mistakes opened up the conversation we'd been having with each other and gave other people a chance to participate. That's the thing with any kind of hobby like this—there's always someone on the internet who loves it a little more than you do. They're a little more obsessed, they're a little better with memorization, and they're super fired up.

At first that realization was intimidating. We'd get emails saying we said the wrong date or left out part of the story or pronounced a city name incorrectly. It felt bad, like we weren't doing our homework correctly. But the messages were always complimentary and fun. That's when we realized that the people communicating with us were excited to be filling us in. Because that's the best part of being into true crime. There's nothing more engaging than talking to someone about a case and finding out they don't know a certain aspect of it.

Now you're the expert! You get to play newscaster and pass on the crucial information like it was passed on to you. It's thrilling and bonding and a great way to pass the time, say, at a Halloween party, for example.

As this podcast grew, we found that not only could we show up as our deeply imperfect selves but that the people who were listening seemed to actually prefer it. The people who were into it wanted our full, sometimes insipid, and sometimes genius conversation, not just the listed facts of terrible crimes. It was a hang. And like any good hang, we felt comfortable confiding in you about all the awful mistakes we'd made in our teens and twenties (and thirties) so you could laugh and say, "I did that!" or wince and say, "I'll never do that!" But we didn't know how huge of a hang it was becoming until we did our first live theater show in Chicago.

We'd been booked at the Athenaeum Theatre for the Chicago Podcast Festival. We either didn't ask how many people it held or we just weren't paying attention, but when our theme song started and we walked out onstage, the ovation was overwhelming. Suddenly, a bunch of people who'd been silently hanging out with us all that time got to let us know that they were there. It was REAL loud. And it was totally thrilling.

We had no idea what we were doing, and it didn't matter. That audience was there for the hang, and they let us know how happy it made them. It was such a moving experience that at the end of that show, to express our gratitude, we invited everyone to meet us in the lobby and say hi after. And they did. We ended up meeting around six hundred people that night. The staff was probably not thrilled with that bit of improvisation, but they accommodated us all beautifully and worked overtime to make it happen. And that was the first night that we got to meet a faction of the Murderino community. And they told us they loved us and that we were doing it right. You can imagine our surprise.

So now we've written this book about some of the themes we come back to again and again on the show and what it all means to both of us. It's kinda personal and it's kinda messy. Let us know if we get anything wrong.

Athenaeum Theatre, Chicago, November 2016

art by Danyell Adams

1

FUCK POLITENESS

GEORGIA: It's all about avoiding the Feeling. You're familiar with the Feeling. It's the regretful, upset, disappointed feeling you get after someone says or does something particularly shitty and you're so taken off guard that your politeness instincts take over so you just ignore it or go with it or kind of shut down. And then later you imagine all the awesome things you could have said or done—all the perfect angles* that you could have kicked that person in the shin—and then you're awake at 3:00 A.M. totally mad at yourself for not having said/done/kicked them. The epitome of fucking politeness is learning how to act in the moment, instead of wishing you had later.

But for women, it's so much more than that. The politeness that we're raised to prioritize, first and foremost, against our better judgment and whether we feel like being polite or not, is the perfect systematically ingrained personality trait for manipulative, controlling people to exploit. We ignore a catcall and seethe inside instead of

---

*   angels

telling the guy to fuck right off. We don't blow off the dude at the bar who's aggressively hitting on us. And we find ourselves in uncomfortable or straight-up dangerous situations that we absolutely do not want to be in and sometimes don't even know how we got into them. All because being rude is so much harder and scarier than being staunch.

Georgia's Take on Red Flags and Riot Grrrl Courage

Little girls are taught to be polite, to smile pretty and sit up straight, to be nice and accommodating. And then those little girls turn into grown-ass women who've spent years being polite to the detriment of their own wants, needs, and safety. Having been one of those little girls who was taught those rules myself, I'm fucking sick of it. So how's about we kick things off with some thoughts on one of our favorite Murderino battle cries: "Fuck politeness." Fuck the way we were socialized. Fuck the expectation that we always put other people's needs first. And while we're at it, fuck the patriarchy! Yeah, I said it.

But fucking politeness is so much easier said than done, and it's taken me years of practice to even start getting the hang of it after a lifetime of being nice.

In July 1998, about a month after my high school graduation, I escaped the confines of my cloyingly suburban hometown in Orange County, California. I graduated by the skin of my teeth. So much so that when the principal handed me my diploma onstage, he gave me a shit-eating grin and said, "Who'd have thunk it?" Through clenched teeth, I did what I was taught to do: I smiled politely as I accepted my hard-won diploma.

I'd been dreaming of being done with public education and escaping all its bullshit rules since I got detention for yawning too loud when

I was in kindergarten, so the dream of college was one I was happy to have neither the academic nor the financial resources to obtain. Instead I moved forty-five minutes away to the sprawling, gritty, insane world that is Los Angeles.

LA had always felt like my real hometown. And not just because I was born there, but I have real roots there. When you live in a transient city like Los Angeles, you tend to meet a lot of people at comedy parties who moved here from wholesome Midwest towns to pursue improv classes, and they can't even fathom that someone would not only be born in Los Angeles but actually raised there as well; you get asked where you're from a lot. My answer is never simple, mostly because saying I grew up in Orange County feels off, like the feeling of sitting in the back seat of your own car. My heart is from Los Angeles and I sprang from my mom's womb in Los Angeles (ew), but I didn't grow up here.

My great-grandparents had emigrated from Eastern Europe to the still-farmland-studded neighboring outskirts of Los Angeles called Boyle Heights, along with a ton of other Jewish immigrants in the 1920s. Later, my grandparents on both sides owned businesses in the equally Jewish-laden Fairfax district, a butcher shop and a barbershop, and my parents went to high school together at Fairfax High on Melrose Avenue. (My once favorite street for vintage shopping.) (More on that later.) But back to the summer of 1998 when I moved into my sweet grandma's midcentury duplex in mid-city where my mother had grown up and I signed up for beauty school.

After eighteen years, I was finally free! I was a grown-up, goddamn it! And I was confident my chutzpah and tenacity would get me through anything. Eighteen-year-olds are stupid that way.

To pay for beauty school classes, I got a job waiting tables at a cute little breakfast spot in Santa Monica that specialized in various pancake situations. Being a waitress always felt like such an "adult" job, and I loved it immediately despite the country theme that made wearing overalls an employment requirement. Nobody looks good in overalls. Except maybe Chrissy Teigen, and even then she'd be like, "Fuck this shit."

I worked the breakfast shift, which meant early morning beach weather, so warm, but overcast and cloudy. It gave the restaurant a cozy, homey vibe, until the marine layer burned off midafternoon and was replaced by that glorious Southern California sunshine that burns brightly despite the smog and exhaust that're slowly killing us all, a fair trade-off for 360 days of sunshine.

I'd drink cup after cup of burned black coffee, and I became friendly with the cook who took pity on my overcaffeinated and underfed body so he'd always sneak me a huge blueberry waffle with a side of extra-crispy bacon to take home at the end of my shift.

And when I say underfed, I mean it was the '90s in LA and I wasn't eating. But truthfully, it wasn't due to the '90s or LA, although I wish I could just blame the time and place. Blaming inanimate stuff is so much easier than taking responsibility for your actions! My eating disorder has been a lifelong affliction, even though I didn't know starving yourself to be prettier was a problem or abnormal until I was much older. I grew up with the typical suburban WASP ethos of: a woman's job is to make men love her or else she's worthless, and men only love women who are beautiful and thin and don't complain a lot. Suburban WASPs don't spell it out like that, but if you've watched one episode of *The Real Housewives of Wherever the Fuck*, you know it's basically their motto. So at eight years old, I was alarmingly skinny. The kids at school called me "the Ethiopian." Hurtful and culturally insensitive at the same time! Kids are so clever!

In my tiny still-forming mind, there was nothing worse than gaining weight. Where did little kid Georgia learn such bullshit? Cut to my mother's room: She's standing naked in front of the mirror and grabbing a handful of her soft belly. I'm right there, and she calls herself "fat" with absolute disgust dripping from her voice. I watched her hate her body, and it's impossible for an eight-year-old not to pick up on that type of behavior. And society was fucking brutal to her because not only did she DARE to have a body with curves, but she was . . . (looks left, looks right, lowers voice) . . . *a single mother.* The nerve! And her socially unacceptable single mother–ness resulted in isolated loneliness that she was told, like all women, to blame on her body.

Consider yourself lucky if you never joined the club of kids from broken homes who had the unsettling experience of being privy to our parents' dating lives. For most of us card-carrying members, it was our first glimpse of how human our parents actually are, an earth-shattering realization at any age.

My parents divorced when I was five, so I had front-row seats to my mother's dating life. I'd best describe her style as "I Need to Find a Husband or I'm Going to Turn into a Witch and Be Burned at the Stake." My mother was (still is) a timeless beauty—she's also smart and funny—but when she was dating someone, I'd watch her turn werewolf-style from a competent, determined authority figure into this entirely not-her version of herself: a desperate, overly flirtatious, subservient ding-dong for shitty men who'd inevitably dump her and leave her in tears. And yes, this is harsh, but this type of personality-corrupting toxic masculinity bullshit didn't spring up from within her out of nowhere. She was taught to do this, taught that acting sweet, deferential, and noncombative was her best chance at securing a man, aka happiness.

I watched her cycle through emotionally unavailable single fathers with mustaches and Volvos. They all promised her the world and charmed the crap out of her by being nice to her weird kids: Asher, Leah, and the angelic youngest . . . me. But eventually all those dads realized we were a hot-mess family of hyperactive neediness that presented itself as a bottomless abyss full of red wine (Mom) and daddy issues (us) (and maybe Mom, but let's not go there).

And hey, just so you don't feel bad for her, one of those emotionally unavailable single fathers with a Volvo became emotionally available and stuck around. She's been with John for fifteen years, and all us hyperactive kids adore him.

When dudes started paying attention to me around junior high, I mimicked the behavior that was modeled to me: egregious availability and an open willingness to do anything for affection. I used to be so embarrassed about how I lost my virginity that I lied about it to everyone who asked, even guys I dated, through my twenties. I always wished I had a sweet, romantic "losing my virginity" story, but that's just not how things go sometimes.

The decisions I made back then about sex and drugs (see "Georgia Gets Her Nipple Pierced for All the Right Reasons") didn't come from a place of self-care and growth. Those were foreign concepts.

It was a dark time. Most of my decisions came from a place of believing the garbage that found its way into my head that, despite ample evidence otherwise, insisted I was ugly, stupid, and worthless. And that narrative told me I didn't have the right to take things slow, or insist we use a condom, or even to just say, "Stop."

That self-advocacy stuff wasn't for girls like me, girls who were taught that their worthiness was determined by who was in love with them.

Quick break from the super dark shit to say: don't worry! Loving myself and deciding my own worth were concepts I finally learned after many mistakes, and billions of hours of therapy (see "Georgia's Top Ten 'Holy Shit!' Moments in Therapy"). I'm like 99 percent healed now.

By the time I turned sixteen, I'd started to find confidence by embracing my inherent weirdness. The angry, in-your-face defiance of my local punk movement helped. I wore Doc Martens and torn-up tights, and one morning before school, I pierced my eyebrow with a safety pin because *fuck you, that's why.* I found other misfits from broken homes who were sick of trying to fit into our cookie-cutter suburb town where everything was painted different shades of beige and eggshell, and together we all reveled in being outcasts.

This one Saturday afternoon, I went with my lifelong next-door neighbor Sanaz, a dreadlocked hippie who wore patchouli oil in lieu of deodorant, to a fund-raising event for Food Not Bombs. It was at my favorite local music venue, Koo's Café (RIP). Koo's was essentially just a dilapidated two-bedroom craftsman house in a bad part of Orange County. Looking back, I really should have died there. Such a fire hazard. But at sixteen, it was a mecca . . . a mold-infested, decaying mecca.

Touring and local bands would play in the bare living room where you'd sweat and shout-sing along, then head out to the front yard to smoke bad weed and talk shit. On the day of the charity, there was a spoken word show, and I wandered in while a girl from the Seattle punk scene spoke to a small crowd sitting cross-legged in front of her, like a classroom of children. She wore the mid-'90s grunge uniform, an oversized flannel over a cute baby-doll dress and ripped tights, kid barrettes in her ratty hair and too much eyeliner, an old tin superhero lunch box as a purse.

She talked about female empowerment. That women were capable and deserving of so much more than the subservient mind-set we were taught to adopt. That if wanting and striving for *more* made you a "bitch," then so be it. That *feminism* wasn't a bad word; it was a vital pursuit and would be until girls were raised to believe in themselves and the importance of their contribution to the world the same way boys were.

It was feminism, which I'd been led to believe was a bad word at the time, but delivered in a punk rock package. They called it Riot Grrrl. Fun fact: one of the origins of the name of the movement was based on the fact that if men were treated for one second the way women have been treated throughout history, there would be a riot. I was on fucking board.

After a childhood of low self-esteem and kowtowing to exclusionary popular girls with starter credit cards and a strict preppy dress code, I gratefully adopted the punk rock female empowerment message

I so desperately needed. I read third-wave feminist zines and binge-listened to "girls to the front" bands like Bikini Kill and Sleater-Kinney.

The confident version of myself buried deep down shook her fist in triumph and I finally started to *like* myself, which was a brand-new sensation. I embraced all the things I had once hated about myself—my hyperactive weirdness, my flat chest—and stopped needing to be liked by other people to the detriment of my own power.

Eventually I graduated high school, moved to LA, and I felt un-fuckwithable. I'd made some new friends in beauty school and started waiting tables at the breakfast spot in Santa Monica. Soon enough I was part of a work family, which included a few regular customers I eventually knew by name and, more intimately, by their regular order.

Lawrence was one of those regulars. We'd joke around a lot during those slow, overcast weekday mornings. He was an older guy, maybe fiftyish, and heavyset with a deep voice. He was like three times my size but had a gentle demeanor. He just came off as this genuinely sweet guy that lived with and took care of his elderly mother. His regular order: over-easy eggs and bacon with a short stack of blueberry pancakes, fortified with tons of coffee. He'd grown up in the neighborhood, and the other waitresses seemed to adore him. He told me he was a professional photographer, so on a particularly slow morning, I asked him if I could take a look at the large portfolio he always carried under his arm. He gestured for me to sit next to him at his usual counter seat. I wiped up a spill of coffee and syrup from the countertop and he opened the large black leather book to show me his photographs.

They were gorgeous. A mix of the touristy yet seedy neighborhoods that made up the beach town he'd always called home. The shots were framed and lit in a way that evoked the dreariness of an overcast oceanside morning, but with a focus on the humanity of his subjects. Through Lawrence's lens, the rude old asshole always standing outside his gaudy jewelry store on the promenade, who'd only take the wet cigar out of his mouth long enough to catcall, became a contemplative represen- tation of hope and community.

So you can imagine how honored I felt when he closed his portfo- lio and asked if he could photograph me sometime.

Look. I know what you're thinking, and you don't have to say it because I'm already yelling it at nineteen-year-old Georgia, the girl who thought she'd outgrown naïveté. I've been yelling it for years: "A dude you barely know asking to photograph you is a HUGE. RED. FLAG."

Look. Listen. The Riot Grrrl in me was screaming in protest at the obvious creepiness of it all, but the little girl in me who's my mother's daughter was flattered and said OK.

On the day of the shoot, I showed up, not because it would have been rude to decline; yeah, it was a little creepy, but I was *excited* to have my picture taken! The idea of fucking politeness hadn't occurred to me because I wasn't being polite, I was looking forward to it. And in an effort to make sure that Lawrence wouldn't have second thoughts once he got a good look at me outside the café walls (a.k.a. in something other than overalls), I'd dressed up for the occasion. I put on a tight, ruffly top with a cherry blossom pattern, capri pants, and way too much makeup. To fake some height, I wore my very '90s platform sandals, which were super in at the time despite the fact that they regularly made your ankle twist out from under you and toppled you to the ground. I threw on a choker and doused myself in glittery apple-scented body spray. I was basically a Gwen Stefani / Spice Girl hybrid and I was Feel- ing. My. Self.

Lawrence and I planned to meet at the café. I figured we'd walk around the neighborhood using the storefronts and graffitied walls as a backdrop, but when I got there, he was waiting out front in his car. He motioned for me to hop in. Into his car. Alone with him.

Hello, red flag number two, thank you for joining us!

But nineteen-year-old Georgia didn't even see that red flag. Without an objection or question, I got in. It turns out a couple of years of confidence and self-esteem weren't enough to override my basic instinct to go along with whatever the guy I'm with is requesting.

Have you ever been in a car that just made you *sad*? His car was basically a man-child on wheels. It wasn't that it was an old car—my car was an ancient hand-me-down that I loved—it was the vibe of the car that made my heart sink, and *that* was my first real jolt of red-flag realization. A vibe.

Trash was everywhere, and the upholstery was stained and frayed. The cloth on the ceiling of the car was stained and ripped. How do you even rip the ceiling of a car?? And it had this musk reminiscent of my brother's room when he was a kid. It's that bad breath, farty male smell that builds up around unshowered men when they never open a window (guys, you know what I'm talking about). Add to that the sweatpants and dirty white T-shirt Lawrence was wearing. Had he always dressed so slovenly? I'd never noticed it in the safety and familiarity of the café.

But, and here it is, I didn't want to hurt his feelings. I didn't want to be an elitist by judging him or his car, so I told him how excited I was and just smiled politely. Maybe I was even trying to convince myself at that point, trying to crowd out those doubts and reservations I was having by using fierce optimism. Cut to me screaming, "Everything is fine!" at a charging bear.

Plus it was too late, right? (Wrong, that's the politeness talking, but I couldn't see it at the time.) I was in his car and he'd already suggested, or really, informed me, that there's a perfect lookout point in the Santa Monica Mountains so we could use the ocean as our backdrop, and by then, we were already winding our way up a narrow two-lane road into the hills.

As we wound up the empty road, gravel crunching under his frayed tires, it truly hit me what a huge mistake I'd made. I was in a strange man's car, all alone, with no way to let anyone know where we were heading. The now-common practice of faking an emergency text from a friend wasn't possible because this was the late '90s, kids. Cell phones were new and not affordable on a waitress salary.

I was stuck, with the mountaintop looming ahead and any change of mind far back in the past. I hadn't told anyone about this photo shoot, and looking back, it must have been because deep down I knew. I knew it was a mistake and that whomever I told would've called me on it and then I would have to tell Lawrence that I couldn't go with him and he'd think I was a jerk. Better to just pretend everything is fine than have an awkward moment and someone thinking badly of me!

My hands clammed up and my heart raced, and my normal nervous habit of talking a mile a minute took over.

I tried to take hold of the situation by using my secret weapons: my Riot Grrrl confidence and the tactics I had learned from my already years-long true-crime obsession. I had picked up tons of questionable survival techniques from watching overly dramatized reenactments on *America's Most Wanted* and terrible Lifetime movies where stalkers had to be fought off in life-or-death battles and abusive husbands always got their comeuppance. I fortified those shows with real-life accounts of survival in books from our true-crime lord and savior, Ann Rule.

In my mind I opened up my toolbox of survival tricks and grabbed at the first one I found: tell him more about yourself so he'll see you as human, which will probably make him less likely to want to hurt you. Humanize yourself but make it kinda tragic so you don't seem like a snob.

At rapid speed, I prattled off my tragic ancestry: Jews from Eastern Europe who had to leave behind everything they owned to escape persecution and after years of being nomads and almost dying all the time finally immigrated to America and made a pretty OK life for themselves with hard work and gusto. I'm the result of the American Dream! You can't murder the American Dream!

Just as I was getting into the darkest details of my foray into meth and rehab, we were pulling over at the intended crime sc—errr, photo shoot location.

We got out of the car and I meekly followed Lawrence up a trail away from the main road, keeping a few extra paces behind but wishing I could turn and run.

It really was a beautiful spot, though. It was a sunny, balmy day, and the sound of the ocean was calming and familiar. At the top of the trail was a sharp cliff that looked over the Pacific Coast Highway, and far out into the ocean I could just see the silhouette of Catalina Island.

To the left was the Santa Monica Pier and its towering Ferris wheel that I had only been on once, when I was a kid with my father, and although it wasn't in sight, I knew that up the coast about twenty minutes to the right was the Jewish camp that I had attended every summer during my childhood. How tragic, I thought, that I was going to maybe possibly probably die in the same mountains where I used to sing camp songs about Israel.

Once again, in my mind it was too late. There was no turning back at that point. I know now that no matter how far into something you are, how many times you've agreed and moved forward, you can *always* decide to turn back. It's often not easy or comfortable, but you get to choose. But back in the mountains, I was just starting to grow my "fuck politeness" wings; they hadn't yet fully developed, and so I thought that I was obligated to stay and deal with the situation I was in. I'd gotten myself into that mess, so it was mine to suffer through. Maybe if I had a little more confidence, or if cell phones and Uber were a thing, I would have felt better about making an excuse and leaving, but probably not.

How insane would it look if I turned and ran down the mountain screaming? Plus, he hadn't done anything wrong yet, right? I was just being paranoid, right?? So I decided to ignore my gut and go with the flow.

He told me to stand with my back to the ocean, and as he got his camera equipment ready, I took some deep breaths to try to calm down. I spotted some surfers bobbing on the waves below and thought of how much I'd rather be there, down on the beach, than stuck on this secluded mountaintop with a grown man I hardly knew.

With a jolt, the name Linda Sobek came to mind. Just a few years earlier, in 1995, the beautiful, kindhearted model had agreed, against her better judgment and her own strict rule of never going alone with a photographer, to accompany freelance photographer Charles Rathbun to a secluded spot on the outskirts of Los Angeles where he brutally raped and murdered her before burying her body in the dirt.

I had followed the trial that had resulted in Rathbun's life sentence, my heart fucking aching for Linda and her family. One decision to trust the wrong person after a career of safe decisions was all it had taken for her life to be put in the hands of a monster. For her to not get a lifetime of experiences because of one moment of not trusting her gut made me so angry. I wondered what she would have said to me if her ghost could visit me on that mountaintop.

When Lawrence put the camera up to his eye, my intuition told me I'd been right to be afraid. It was terrifying. In my life, I've never had a more intuitive, gut feeling that something was off, and I'll never forget it or ignore it again. The eye that didn't look through the camera, the one that was trained on me, went black and scary. An intensity that suddenly matched his size and the problematic request to have a teenage girl alone with him in a secluded spot was evident in his glare. I thought of Linda and all the other girls who'd been fooled into this exact same scenario by countless men over countless decades. I couldn't believe I was staring down the barrel of becoming one of the unlucky ones who fell for the trick of a seemingly gentle man who turned out to be a monster, all because I had dismissed so many opportunities to trust my gut and fuck politeness.

Twenty-three-year-old Janice Ott helped a handsome man with his arm in a sling who turned out to be Ted Bundy. Nineteen-year-old Judy Ann Dull needed money to fight for custody for her child, so she posed for photos with photographer-turned-serial-killer Harvey Glatman, aka the Glamour Girl Slayer. Both women were tortured and murdered. I've wondered about the exact moment they knew. When vague, ignorable red flags turned into sure knowledge that they were in danger.

The gentle, sweet man I thought I knew was gone the second he trained his camera on me. The man I joked with while busing tables at the café, who loved his mother and real maple syrup on his pancakes and always tipped 20 percent. The man holding the camera was scary and evil. The look on what I could see of his face was dark and soulless. I knew where he was going to take this from that first shot.

Scared and intimidated, I just wanted to get this photo shoot over with and go home. I wanted to wash all my dumb makeup off and put on sensible shoes and act like a sensible girl. I thought I knew better because of my fascination with true crime and that my Riot Grrrl attitude made me immune from danger, but it turns out all the books and ripped tights and baby-doll dresses in the world couldn't keep me from becoming exactly as paralyzed by fear as I swore I never would be.

Instead, I found out how easily even a badass feminist with a head full of cautionary tales could become a victim. How charming people can make us put our guard down and how we're all susceptible to flattery and manipulation.

Lawrence snapped away, glaring at me with his intense one-eyed stare. I just wanted it to be over so we'd leave. I posed and smiled as he instructed, while looking around for somewhere to run in case he advanced on me, but I was at the edge of a cliff, the Pacific Ocean behind me, and this man I knew nothing about, had never had more than a friendly chat with, hulking in front of me blocking my path back to the road.

Just when I thought we were almost done, when he seemed satisfied that he had gotten some good options and I was starting to think that I actually had been overreacting and nothing nefarious was in the stars for me that day, he said, "Why don't you take your top off?"

And that did it, something snapped. I channeled the ghost of Linda Sobek, gathered up all that Riot Grrrl courage, fucked politeness, kicked Lawrence in the dick, stole his sad car, and got the fuck out of there!

The end.

OK, no, that's not true. That's what I wish I'd done, but the little girl who was raised to be polite, the girl whose ingrained default setting was acquiescence, and who deep down was truly afraid of what the outcome would be if I said no, that girl kicked the Riot Grrrl off the cliff, and after that, fucking politeness didn't seem like an option anymore. Or at least didn't feel like the smart, safe option.

I should have listened to my gut way back before we got to the part where he thought he could ask me to take my top off. The rudeness and awkwardness I would have felt when I insisted that he pull over and let me out of the car way back at the bottom of the mountain would have been a much more comfortable experience than the one I was in now. The one that didn't have options. But I had essentially been my own horrible friend by telling myself to calm the fuck down and rolling my eyes at my paranoia. If an actual friend had come to me with this, I would have told them to get the fuck out of there. I would have taken them seriously. Why wasn't I that generous with my own feelings?

I still wonder what would have happened if I had refused to take off my top and demanded we leave immediately rather than let him take photos of me and my perky tits at the top of the Santa Monica mountains with Catalina Island just visible in the background. But I'll never know because I obliged out of fear and intimidation. There was a part of me that felt like this is what I deserved, to be objectified and humiliated. What did I *think* was going to happen when I had said yes to this?

I felt numb and in shock, like someone else was inhabiting my body. I peeled off my blouse with the cherry blossom print and ruffles around the sleeves and tossed it aside onto the dirt beside my vintage tin lunchbox purse and did the same with my bra when he insisted. As he took photos, I did everything I could not to let the rock in my chest transform into the hot, humiliated tears that were on the verge of spilling over.

When he finished snapping photos, I slipped my shirt back on and stuffed my bra in my back pocket. I've never been so happy to have a shirt on. My tits were now on a roll of film in his camera and he could do whatever he wanted with it, but I pushed the thought out of my mind. I was just so embarrassed. I didn't have the capacity to absorb anything else and I was still on high alert, jumping at any action from Lawrence as we made our way to the car.

I talked the entire ride down the mountain and back to the café, shocked at every moment that nothing more was happening. When we *finally* arrived back at the café, I jumped out, got in my car, and locked the doors. A few blocks away, I pulled over and cried with my forehead on the steering wheel, eyeliner running down my face, relief and shame washing over me. Relief that the situation hadn't gotten worse, that he hadn't asked me to undress further or come on to me. Maybe he had planned to do those things but sensed my fear? And what if I'd said no? Would he have gotten angry with me? Worried I'd tell someone that he wanted to take topless pictures of me? Would he have done something to make sure I didn't ruin his good reputation? Going along with what he wanted, being polite and accommodating, it was so much easier than finding out the answer to how he would have reacted to my *no*.

Of course, since then, I've been in countless situations where I've been presented with the opportunity to fuck politeness, and I'm proud to say I've exercised that right with varying degrees of extremism. I'm still proud of myself over this one time a guy I wasn't super close to or comfortable with asked me if I wanted a shot. A bunch of us were hanging out at a bar. It was later in the night and most of my closer friends had gone home. Just a few of us stragglers were still hanging out, soaking up those final few minutes before last call and the subway ride home.

I told him repeatedly that I didn't want a shot. Shots make me go from tipsy to shitfaced faster than you can say, "Regretful one-night stand." I also know that a dude you don't know very well wanting to buy you a shot is—you guessed it!—a red flag, and his insistence despite my firmly saying no was a red flag that was flapping in my face fucking pissing me off.

So, you know where this story goes. He bought me a shot. Because of course he fucking did. And when he handed it to me, he toasted with his own shot. *You have got to be kidding me.* I just stared at him in disbelief while he and some other guy egged me on to shoot this drink I'd made abundantly clear I didn't want. I thought about pre–Riot Grrrl Georgia, who would have taken this shot to show that she was a "cool girl," one who could keep up with the boys and would do so just to be liked.

I wasn't that girl anymore. I was in control of my decisions and therefore my destiny because I believed in myself and had no qualms with being rude in order to keep myself safe. I didn't owe this guy anything. So I smiled politely, looked both dudes pointedly in the eye, held up the drink, and turned the shot glass upside down, spilling its entire contents out all over the sticky bar floor. Then I swooped up my things and split.

Hold for applause

The first time I ever told anyone about my photo shoot with Lawrence was when I told Karen about it on the podcast, over fifteen years later. I didn't even mention taking my shirt off, because I wasn't ready to go there yet. Karen was talking through the story of the asshole rapist and murderer Rodney Alcala who during the '70s convinced hundreds of women that he was a professional fashion photographer and would ask to photograph them for his "portfolio." He took their photos and then raped and murdered them. He was eventually sentenced to death for murdering five women, although his victim count is thought to be much higher.

Karen and I try our best to never blame the victim. Victim blaming is an easy trap to fall into when you've never been in the types of truly horrific situations we discuss. And even as someone who'd been in the *exact same position*, it was hard for me not to wonder why the hell anyone would have gone alone with Alcala in the first place. I needed to actively remind myself that I'd made the same choice; the results just happened to be less murdery.

I think up until I heard Karen talk about the women who agreed to go alone with Alcala to a secluded location under the guise of being photographed, I'd blamed myself for the idiocy that led me to my photo shoot with Lawrence. Again, we make a conscious effort never to victim blame on our podcast, but here I was trashing myself. And you want to know the shittiest part? Deep down I also knew that if I'd actually been attacked by Lawrence, I would have thought it was my fault for putting myself in a situation where it was even a possibility.

A couple of months after I talked to Karen about this whole thing, I finally brought it up with my therapist because I was having such a hard time convincing myself that I wasn't a stupid idiot for going with Lawrence. I felt that I had no right to be mad at him or consider myself a victim in this situation because so much worse had happened to other women who had put themselves in a situation like this.

That's how ashamed I was. I was less embarrassed about letting someone take topless photos of me than I was about letting myself get into a situation I couldn't control. It didn't fit with the strong, feminist persona I was trying so hard to shroud myself in.

But the reality is a grown man gained the trust of a teenage girl and took her to a secluded spot and pressured her into an intimate situation she didn't feel safe saying no to. It took me saying that sentence in therapy to stop being so mean to myself for what happened that day. My therapist asked me if I truly didn't feel there was any blame to be laid on the victims I'd been telling her about: Linda Sobek or Janice Ott or Judy Ann Dull. After a moment of contemplation and introspection—because if I'm gonna be problematically honest with anyone, it's my therapist—I told her the truth: I know that none of those women were to blame in any way for what was done to them.

Sometimes responding to the world and people and difficult situations with bravery and confidence feels impossible. Fucking politeness isn't a strict rule, it's a practice, an art to master throughout your life. Think of it like a weapon you carry in your pocket. With practice (I recommend practicing on dudes in bars who really want to buy you shots) you'll learn to wield that weapon like a fucking ninja in order to protect yourself. Throughout your life, you'll master knowing what situations call for what level of fucking politeness. This is why it's so important to recognize red flags for what they are: warning signals that, when paid attention to, are basically crystal balls into what level of "ga fuck yaself" is necessary.

So here's your takeaway: fuck politeness. Fuck it to whatever degree you think is most appropriate to the severity of the situation. If you were raised to be polite, it'll be hard, but you can totally do it, and you'll feel so empowered once you do. Now, here's the most important part: If you don't fuck politeness, if you struggle to get the words out, or if you can't or won't see the red flags that would alert you to the need to fuck politeness, know this: nothing that happens as a result of your inaction is your fault. Know it. You can't prepare yourself out of being hurt.

It took a while before I came to understand that I was susceptible to predators. And that my Riot Grrrl badassness was great for self-care and my own personal self-image, but that nothing will ever trump the importance of believing in my gut, trusting my intuition, and being kind enough to myself to be rude as fuck to those who didn't deserve my confidence. These are some of the most important things I've learned, and none of them came from a classroom.

Who'd have thunk it?

Karen's Guide to Prioritizing Your Own Agenda

Of all the life-affirming slogans born out of Georgia and I ranting to each other as we discuss true crime, I like Fuck Politeness the best. It's direct, it's catchy, and you get to say *fuck*—a true catchphrase trifecta. But it also encapsulates the worldview I was raised with and one that's served me well over the years. My parents taught me to have a healthy disrespect for authority, so the whole idea of fucking politeness is one that's very close to my heart. And it's one I took for granted, as you do with parents and what's cool about them. This is going to get sad, by the way. Just in case you're not here for that, I figured I'd warn you now. Although I have a feeling that's not going to scare you away. I mean, Georgia's story wasn't exactly a walk in the park and you did just buy a book with the word *murder* in the title.

My mom, Patricia Kilgariff, died on January 9, 2016, twelve years after being diagnosed with early-onset Alzheimer's at the age of sixty-three. It was a long and painful unraveling that pulled my father and sister and me all to pieces. We didn't know what to do with her and we didn't know what to do without her, and we had to cope with both problems at the same time.

This disease runs in families, passed down on the mother's side. My grandma Grace had it, too. She was a hilarious, delighted, devoted grandmother who moved in with us when I was seven. We watched her deteriorate until she finally had to be put into a nightmare convalescent hospital that none of us ever wanted to go to. So on top of the normal pain of watching her slowly disappear, we all felt a massive amount of guilt and shame for not visiting her every day. And then she was gone. What had seemed like an endless heartache was suddenly over. We finally had some closure and some relief, but even that relief felt bad. Then, twenty years later, my mom began to repeat herself and the whole nightmare started up again.

About five years into my mom's diagnosis, a friend at a party asked me how I was doing. My standard reply was something like, "I'm fine. It's harder on my dad and sister since they're home with her." But as I went to say it, a truer thought hit me. I told my friend this: "Having a parent with Alzheimer's is like living inside a horror movie that's playing out in real time. It's as horrifying and awful as it is tedious and mundane. It'd be like if you lived in the movie *Jaws*. You're happily swimming in the ocean and then everyone starts screaming, 'Shark!' You start to panic, but then someone else yells that the shark is twenty miles away, so you calm down a little. But then a third person gets on the bullhorn and says you're not allowed to get out of the water ever again. So you start panicking and flailing and fighting and yelling for help. You scream about how unfair it is, you having to be out in the ocean with this killer shark alone when all those other people get to be on the beach. You scream until your voice is hoarse. No one responds. You finally start to accept that it's your fate. But then you start thinking everything that touches you is the shark. You can't calm down because you can't stop reacting to things that aren't there. You grab wildly at anything that looks like a weapon, but every time, it turns out to be seaweed. Boats go by filled with happy families enjoying the sun. You hate them all so much it makes you feel sick. Then you get really tired and you cry so hard you think your head will burst. And then finally, you gather all your strength and turn to look at the shark. Now it's 19.8 miles away. It's the slowest shark in history, but you know it's coming right for you. And after five years in the water, you start rooting for the fucking shark."

When my little speech was done, we stood in silence. My friend didn't know what to say. What I'd just come out with was heavy and sad, not something you could smile and walk away from. He looked horribly uncomfortable. I felt a wave of embarrassment. I'd overshared a very dark revelation at a low-key, summertime backyard party. But then, my friend Adam, whose father also had Alzheimer's, pushed past my silent friend and grabbed me by the shoulder. "Oh my god, yes! That's EXACTLY what it's like!" We both started laughing and couldn't stop. It felt so good to pin it down and let it out.

After that, I never lied when someone asked me how things were going with my mom. Instead of worrying about the comfort of the person who was asking, I started thinking about whoever might be listening to my answer; all the other people trapped out in the water with that slow, terrible shark.

These days, when the subject of my mom comes up, the first thing that pops into my mind is this five-second memory gif I have of her from a holiday party at our house, circa 1989.

I'd like to state here that practically our entire kitchen was country blue with a goose design. The kitchen tile was country blue, the cookie jar was a goose, the dish towels had country blue piping and showed groups of geese gathered around ponds or standing in groups of twos and threes. This bold choice had been borne out of my mother's desperate desire to break free from her '70s design aesthetic: chickens. She'd let it slip sometime around 1975 that she liked chickens, so from then on, that was all she got. We had paintings of chickens and chicken calendars, chicken corn-on-the-cob holders and chicken serving dishes. I remember watching her opening a gift one Christmas morning and announcing, "If whatever this is has a fucking chicken on it, I'm gonna go insane." My dad got mad that she said the F-word on Christmas. I found the whole moment thrilling. Anyway, when we moved into our new house in the late '80s, my mom got out in front of her chicken infestation and made it clear that she was now all about the country blue goose.*

* It's goddamn hilarious that geese were presented as a symbol of bucolic farm life. Anyone who's spent time with actual geese knows what I mean. They are fucking demons. They look sweet and pretty, and it's easy to mistake them for swans from a distance, but when you approach them, they run at you and hiss and try to bite you with their weird, tiny human teeth. It's like something out of *Pan's Labyrinth*. Stay away.

In this gif, it's Thanksgiving, so our kitchen is filled with Kilgariff aunts and our old next-door neighbors, the Hospodars. (Their farm
had the geese that terrorized my sister and me.) My mom is bustling
around the kitchen in her maroon linen separates, her silk neck scarf
pushed aside by a dirty dish towel thrown over her shoulder. She's
eavesdropping on the nearest conversation as she's pulling an appe-
tizer out of the oven, and as she slams the oven door, she yells, "Oh,
bullshit, Bob!"

It brings a tear to my eye when I think of it now, how my mom never
gave a single shit about what other people thought. She was a real war-
rior: sharp and engaging and a natural contrarian. She thought for
herself and spoke her mind. She loved to debate, defend underdogs,
and lecture everyone on how Ronald Reagan's policies were gutting the
mental health system she'd worked so hard to maintain. As a psychiatric nurse, she understood how complex and difficult some people's
lives could be. She was sensitive and helpful but lived by an overall rule

of tough love and uncomfortable honesty. She was truly the queen of fuck politeness.

My older sister, Laura, is a single mom, and her eyes go wide when she talks about what our mom managed to get done in a day. Putting in twelve to fourteen hours as the head nurse of a psychiatric hospital and then coming home to all of our problems, including what we were having for dinner. Although, to give proper credit, my dad usually cooked. He was a fireman in San Francisco, so he had some serious skills in

 the kitchen. But when he was on duty, it was up to Pat. To this day, I blame her terrible cooking for my love of dry chicken, Minute Rice, as well as giving up and ordering Chinese food. On the days when my dad was at work, my sister and I could go next door to the Hospodars' after school. We'd do chores on the farm, then run around in the creek or the back fields until it got dark. We'd watch TV until my mom came to pick us up.

She'd come in and Aunt Jean and Uncle Steve would pour her a glass of wine, and they'd all sit down and chat. This was what she called Adult Time, which meant we weren't allowed to bother them. For example, if I came out of the TV room crying because my sister just hit me in the head with a large green ashtray, all the adults would say, "It's Adult Time!" and I'd have to wait to be comforted until Adult Time was over. It was almost like a civic ordinance they weren't allowed to break. We always ended up staying for dinner, and afterward, my mom and Aunt Jean would linger for hours around the empty dinner table, drinking wine and smoking cigarettes and cackling together. I think having Aunt Jean next door was the thing that kept my mom sane, and their evening ritual was a very '70s rudimentary form of self-care.

Like a lot of kids back then, we were as spoiled as we were ignored. For years, I had a real resentment about having a working mom. Moms with jobs weren't all that common in our town, and most of our friends' moms were homemakers. It may have even been frowned upon by some of them that she worked full-time. Luckily, my mom wasn't concerned with what the frowners thought. Once, when I told her I wanted her to be friends with my best friend's mom, she replied without looking up from the newspaper, "I already have plenty of friends, honey." I then started crying, saying that it was unfair to me that she wasn't like normal moms and that I never had milk and cookies waiting for me after school. She folded a corner of the paper down, looked at me sympathetically, and said, "Karen, you're being hysterical. You can make cookies anytime you want. You just have to remember to turn the oven off."

My mom was tough, and she knew how to take care of business. She'd been an only child with two alcoholic parents, so she learned very early on how to make her own way in the world. She had these highly refined survival skills paired with beauty and a natural charm. Once, she got stopped by a policeman in my hometown while she was on her way to work. She pulled the car over and immediately got out and walked back to the police car in her white nursing uniform. The cop rolled down his window, and she leaned down and said, "Thank you for pulling me over. I understand I was going over the speed limit, but I'm late for work so I really have to go. Keep up the good work." Then she got back into her car and drove away. Now, I realize this sounds like a family tall tale, but if anyone could do this, it was my mom. She had a couple of things going for her in this situation—first and foremost, she was white. Second of all, the nurse's uniform gave her a kind of authoritarian angel look that you can see in her picture and it was hard to argue with. (Although I did every chance I got.) Plus, my mom had this lilt in her voice that made you feel like she was sharing an inside joke with only you. That's the thing about fuck politeness—it's not about being rude.

One night when my dad was at work, she took my sister and me to a diner called Lyon's. It was kinda like a Denny's but with better chicken strips. On the car ride there, I started to get a headache. By the time we sat down in our booth, my head hurt so bad I had to keep my eyes closed. Like a typical nurse, my mom didn't carry aspirin or any kind of medicine with her, except a soft pack of Benson & Hedges Lights 100s and some loose Velamints. Normally, when I complained about feeling sick, she'd tell me to drink water and stop pouting, and when I did, I'd feel better because I didn't have a choice. But this time, she could tell I was hurting. I winced anytime someone dropped their fork, and the idea of a grilled cheese made me gag.

So when the waitress came, my mom said, "Excuse me, do you have any aspirin or Tylenol that I could buy? My daughter's head is really hurting her."

The waitress made a sympathetic clucking noise and said, "Hold on, let me go check."

When she came back, she spoke in a different, sort of formal voice. "I'm sorry, ma'am. We're legally not allowed to dispense medicine to our customers."

In the same weird formal tone, my mom said, "I understand. Thanks, anyway."

I wanted to cry. Now I was going to have to sit through dinner with my head splitting and my mom didn't even care. I opened my eyes and turned toward her to complain, but as I did, I saw the waitress fold her arms and put her fist out ever so slightly. "Would you like to hear the soups for today?"

Without breaking eye contact, my mom brushed her hand under

the waitress's fist as she replied, "Absolutely." The waitress rattled off three soups and then walked away.

My mom pushed my water glass over to me, placed two aspirin in my hand, and whispered, "Here, honey, take these."

Somehow, my mom had scored me Anacin like a British spy! How did she do that? She sensed that the waitress was lying and then caught on to the aspirin handoff like she did it every day? My sister was sitting a foot away, and she missed the entire exchange. They were speaking in code, both knowing what the other one was truly saying. That night, as my headache lifted, I slowly realized that my mom was a fucking badass.

I'd spent so much time being mad that my mom wasn't like Marion Cunningham. Or any mom on TV for that matter. She wasn't sweet. She didn't make cookies. She was rarely there to ask me how my day was, champ. I thought that meant I was unimportant to her.

That night, I saw that my mom was of the world and in the world, working to make it a better place. And she was doing it for me. My mom knew stuff, like how to pass drugs in a family diner and not blow it. She knew how to get us what we needed without demanding to see the manager. She spoke a subtle human language that connected her to other people in a real way.

My mom talked to people everywhere she went, and she laughed a lot. I always thought my mom knew the cashiers at Clothestime because she'd have these sweet, personal conversations with them while they rang up our outfits. She'd be exhausted from work and irritated that I was spending two hours trying to find a dress exactly like Pat Benatar's in the "Love Is a Battlefield" video. But when I finally gave up and we'd get to the register, my mom always chatted with the cashier. She'd ask how their day had been and really listen to their answer. Usually, the whole encounter would end with both of them laughing and my mom giving the girl a wink. On the way to the car, I'd ask, "Who was that lady?" thinking my mom must've known her from town. But she'd always say, "What do you mean, honey? She works there."

I have another gif memory of my mom in my head, but it's a sad one. And it's not even one of my memories. It's from a story my sister told me. But I can see it so clearly.

When the Alzheimer's had really begun to take hold, my mom spent her days submerged in confusion, constantly anxious and defiant and sometimes embarrassingly childish. She'd pretend to follow along when the rest of us were talking, but when she tried to add something, it'd be disconnected and unnerving. This was the hardest time, when she was not totally gone and yet not there at all. Sometimes she'd say something really mean, and before I could stop myself, I'd respond with an equally shitty remark. Then she'd look surprised and sad and ask me why I was mad at her. It was like she was gaslighting us backward, and it was pure hell. My sister and I finally came up with a code. When one of us was reacting to the crazy things she'd say, the other one would yell, "Swiss cheese!" as a reminder that we were mad at a person whose brain was filled with holes, like Swiss cheese. It helped a little. Like on that one Easter, when she told everyone in a loud voice that she'd never wanted kids. All three of my aunts sitting closest to her began talking at the same time, as if they could somehow cover up my mom's big reveal with noise and words. I was heartbroken. My sister looked over at me and shrugged. "Hey, Swiss cheese, right?"

That Christmas, I came home to visit and stayed with my mom while my dad went to play golf. It was maybe five hours total, and it felt like a year. She was crabby and nervous and constantly asking where my father was. The moments dragged on. I told myself to be strong and make the most of the very little time I had left with my very sick mother, but every moment I spent with her proved that she was just an impostor.

At one point, she told me she needed to take a nap, so I brought her upstairs and helped her get under the covers. Suddenly, she forgot what we were doing and started fighting me. In a weird whiny voice, she said she didn't want to go to bed. She told me to get away from her and tried to slap me. I couldn't handle it anymore. I screamed that I was just trying to help her, why did she have to be so awful. She looked confused for a second, then her entire face dropped and she began to stutter an apology, begging me not to be mad at her. It was horrifying.

By the time my dad got home, I was a total mess. My sister came to get me, and I cried all the way back to her house. When I finally calmed down, I admitted that I'd yelled at Mom and scared her. And then I started crying so hard I thought I was going to throw up. My sister rubbed my back for a bit, and then she told me the story that planted the sad gif memory in my brain. She said, "That same thing happened to me once. Just like that. I was trying to get her into bed and she was being really mean, so I was being mean back, but then I just started crying. It felt so crazy and awful and I was so tired. And then, right in the middle of all of it, Mom grabbed me by the arm and pulled me toward her, and I swear to god, she came back. It was normal Mom. She was there. I could see it was her in her eyes. She just looked at me and said in her regular voice, 'You do know how much I loved both of you, don't you?' She came back so she could tell me that. That's how great our mom was."

My mom's life was a victory. She didn't suffer fools, even when they were her own children, and she always questioned authority. She wasn't aggressive or self-righteous; she was just a no-shit gal. She did what she thought was best. She was grateful every day for the life she built, and she tried to share that gratitude with others, in case they weren't as lucky as she was. She knew how hard life could be, so she celebrated every good moment. And she always had a sparkle in her eye.

I think part of that was because she knew she could get Alzheimer's. She was a nurse, she knew it was a hereditary disease, and she was aware that she was on a clock. And that's true for all of us. We barely get any time on this planet. Do not spend it pleasing other people. Fuck politeness. Live life exactly how you want to live it so you can love the life you make for yourself. Make Pat proud.

Fuck Politeness: Final Thoughts

GEORGIA: Why do you think this idea resonated with so many Murderinos?

KAREN: I think our listeners like the phrase *Fuck Politeness* because (a) there's swearing and (b) it's what everyone wants to do but has been led to believe they're not allowed to do. We're giving you the permission to act in your own best interests before considering anyone else's.

GEORGIA: What's the difference between politeness and kindness?

KAREN: Basically, as long as you weren't raised by wolves, anyone can be polite. You can hate someone's guts and still say all the things you're supposed to say in a civil exchange. Politeness doesn't require actual humanity. It's just cultural ritual. Kindness means you actually care and have good intentions toward a person. It means you think about them as much as you think about yourself.

Politeness is fancy curtains in your front window. Kindness is the home-cooked meal on your dinner table.

GEORGIA: Fucking politeness can be super awkward and uncomfortable or make you feel like a dick. How do you get over this and do what's right for you despite that?

KAREN: Let's be clear: the idea of fucking politeness isn't about standing on a corner shouting, "Fuck you!" to anyone passing by. It's a strategy for when someone tries to invade your space somehow. They started it. They're the dick here. You're just fighting fire with fire. You can't care what a dick thinks about you. They rely on that fear of judgment to keep you in their control. I always think it's good just to say what you're thinking aloud. Some guy comes up to you on the street and starts asking you a bunch of personal questions, you can say to him, "Whoa, this is weird behavior. I don't know you at all. You seem like a predator. Goodbye." If he gets mad and yells, "Bitch!" at you, that doesn't mean you're a bitch. It means you were right.

art by Haley D. Fischer of Elle.Dot Studio

2

SWEET BABY ANGEL

GEORGIA: We're all born sweet baby angels. Darling little cooing, farting babies that haven't got an evil bone or bad intention present. And then life happens to us, and some of us lose that sweet-baby-angel sheen and become harder, badder, and our halos crack or rust.

A sweet baby angel can be many things:

- A person who doesn't expect bad things to happen to them. They aren't on the lookout for red flags, and they never think they might get murdered. They don't read or watch true crime. They aren't preoccupied with morbid things. They are probably young, innocent, and happy to help strangers with groceries. They act in a way that people should act in an ideal world. Then when a sweet baby angel starts to learn things about violence and cruelty, they become a Murderino.
- People who are good at the core. They may know about the worst parts in life, they might even be obsessed with true

crime, but they still think the world is worth saving and they want to use their powers of anxiety for good.

- An innocent who doesn't deserve the bad thing that happened to them.

Karen's Lecture on Self-Care

As we begin, picture me dragging a chair across the floor of the imaginary classroom we're now in together, slamming it down, and sitting in it backward. That's right, I'm about to relate to you on a deep, mid-'90s, *Dangerous Minds* level. You might not be ready. I see you crossing your arms and squinching up your face, knowing there's nothing I can teach you that you haven't already learned in this accredited junior college we call real life. Maybe that's true. But I've already turned my Kangol hat logo-forward so I have no choice but to school you.

Now I'm writing on the chalkboard. SELF . . . (it always takes forever when a teacher writes anything on a chalkboard in a movie) . . . CARE. Hard dot at the end even though a period doesn't belong there. Then an underline. <u>SELF-CARE</u>. What is it? I believe self-care is a concept Oprah invented after her thyroid exploded and she was forced to take two weeks off. But it's really taken off as a concept in recent years. How do we treat ourselves in the day to day, and how does that treatment impact our lives? These questions essentially disqualify me from speaking on the subject. Unlike the authors of all the self-care articles I've read over the years, I am not a petite young vegan with radiant skin who swears by meditation and ghee. I've only driven through Sedona, and I'm literally scared to take a hot yoga class. It just seems too hot. So what could I possibly teach you about self-care?

This is where I whip the piece of chalk at you and it hits you in the forehead, making you sit up and take notice. I'm going to explain to you how self-care isn't about you. Long pause. I scan the room with so much self-satisfied staring. That's right. It ISN'T about you. Cue "Gangsta's Paradise" as I kick my chair over.

Now before I explain what I mean, if you're the rare bird who's chill and lets things go and is a basically happy person most of the time, you can fuck right on outta this chapter. There's nothing for you here. Oh, wait! If you put lemon juice on your face, it fades your freckles. Then again, I bet your freckles look really good on you and you know it, and that's part of why you're so chill. Again, my words cannot help you. Kindly see your way to the exit of the book.

Also, if you've always been popular, attractive, and sought after, none of this will make sense to you. You are a unicorn. Go lock yourself in a castle on a high hill.

Related to that, if you're one of those women who says that you've only had guy friends because you're so pretty all women are jealous of you, put this book down and go to therapy immediately. Not only will this chapter confuse you, but you are lying to yourself in a terrible way. Stop blaming, get honest, and fix your shit. And then when you're done, make some actual female friends. You need them very badly.

Most importantly, if you have clinical depression, I'm not qualified to help you, but lots of people are and really want to, so definitely go get a slice of that ASAP. You deserve to be happy, no matter what your brain tells you.

Now that they're gone, the real people can get real. I'm talking about the fuckups and the drama queens, the ones who get told they're too much: too big, too loud, too smart, too mean. I'm talking to the people who have been severely scraped up by life and by the mistakes they've made in it. You guys are my favorite because you are me and I am you.

I assume you're over twenty if you're reading this book (if not, hi! What are you doing up so late on a school night? None of this applies to you, you nut. Go read the Great Brain series by John D. Fitzgerald instead. You'll love it), and chances are you're either in the middle of some kind of personal drama—you're in a huge fight with your mom, your best friend caught you talking shit behind her back, you're in unrequited love with your married boss, you know the kind of drama I mean— or you're just wrapping some up and in the market for more. Let me stop you for one moment and say: QUIT IT.

Don't get into a fight with one more friend over the umbrella they borrowed and never gave back or the time they didn't save you a seat at the group dinner or whatever the fuck. Stop finding fault and making a fuss and crying in weird apartment building hallways expecting people to come out and wrap you up in a warm blanket of giving a shit. They're not going to. Yes, it would be really nice, but it's unrealistic to the point of self-abuse. Everyone has their own problems. Some of them are awful and tragic, and if you knew what they were, you'd be grateful for the ones you have.

And be honest with yourself; the problems you have are yours. No matter who came into play before, during, or after, you are the common denominator. Now HOLD ON! This is not to say that you're always to blame for what happens to you. That would be dumb and mean and kind of Republican. What I'm saying is: you're responsible for your own quality of life. Accepting that fact is the first step in the journey to that distant oasis that is watered by the ancient spring of self-care.

I recommend taking this step with a licensed therapist. They know the path, and they're good at getting you back onto it when you go wandering into the dunes of anger and blame and self-righteous storytelling. I know it sounds hard to ask for psychiatric help, but it really isn't. Everyone's doing it! And OH MY GOD does it help.

I avoided therapy for years and years. I waited until my life was total shit, and then I waited four more months. At the time, I was working in an incredibly high-pressure, all-consuming job that I hated and felt trapped in. I was so busy with said job, I stopped doing comedy altogether. My mom had been diagnosed with Alzheimer's two years before (and you know how that was going for me—the slow-shark scenario had just begun). My dad had just found out he had a patch of melanoma on his scalp that the doctors feared had moved into his brain. So you could say it wasn't a fun time for me.

Then one day, I noticed a pattern. Every time something bad happened at work, I'd rant to a coworker about whose fault it was. I'd go on and on about how much I hated the guilty party, and then I'd feel awful. The guilt would eat me up. Soon, I'd hate the person I'd just confided in. And the next day, the monologue would start again. Only the names would change.

When it hit me that I was doing this, I knew I was in serious trouble. Luckily, I found my therapist soon after and told her about my realization. That's when she dropped the bomb about having too many "friends." This concept is fully explained in "Karen on How to Not Drink the Kool-Aid Even When You're Spiritually Parched," but the short version is: don't throw your shit all over town. If you have a problem, don't just confide in whoever wanders into your office. Save it for a person who cares about your well-being. We all have a handful of friends like that. Figure out who your clutch-five friends are and drop your expectations of everyone else.

Here's a good example of how a clutch-five friend works: The other night, I had dinner with my friend Lizzy, who I love and who is very deep and wise. We're both comedians, writers, and spiritual seekers, and we like to get together every couple of weeks and sit in a restaurant talking and laughing until it closes around us. We discuss every single thing we can think of that's interesting or juicy, and we give each other feedback about our current worries and sadnesses. *Sadnesses* is too a word! I don't care what you say, spellcheck.

So this one particular night, we were having one of our talk-down dinners, but I could feel the flow was off. She'd ask me about things she knew were going on in my life, but when I'd update her on them, she'd look kind of worried, say something pat, and change the subject.

At first, it was confusing. Normally I could say the most insane thing and she'd unconditionally support and explore it. Once, while I was loudly recounting a text exchange I'd just had with a guy I liked, I caught something out of the corner of my eye. I stopped talking and froze in a panic. She saw my face drop and asked what was wrong. As quietly as I could, I whispered, "Oh my god, Lizzy, I think he's sitting at the next table." Without another word, she casually reached over for her purse and snuck a look at every person sitting next to us. She turned back and said quietly, "Unless he's a bald man in his late sixties, it's not him." I almost cried with relief not just because I didn't get caught but because she immediately had my back without question or judgment. My shame lifted. We ordered dessert, and I told the story again, even louder.

That's why, on this night, her lack of acceptance was hitting me so hard. I assumed I was being too negative. But she was the one asking! And I was just giving her the facts. But I went with every subject change, trying to be honest but ultimately positive. Still, her reaction was the same. I started to get frustrated. This wasn't how we did things. Something was going on.

Now pre-therapy me would've been so hurt and shamed that I would've sunk into a pouty silence and waited until she spoke so I could do the same thing back to her. But because I'm old and wise and therapized—yes that IS a word, spellcheck, you fucking narc—I didn't let it slide.

Me, dropping my french fry for dramatic effect: "I'm sorry, I have to tell you, it feels like you don't want to hear anything I'm saying."

Her, suddenly thrilled: "Thank you for being honest. I could tell something was bugging you."

Me, upset, fryless: "I just feel like I'm bumming you out."

Her, pushing her blue-corn waffle aside: "To be honest, I'm going through some hard things right now, and I feel like I need to keep myself up and happy. When the vibrations get low, I think I panic and want to run away."

And look (listen), she's right. It's much easier for me, for all of us, to complain and gossip because it holds the listener's interest, but it does have a negative residual effect. I thought I was making fun dinner conversation, but it was actually just a release for me. My friend had no choice but to open up those "low vibrational" topics because that's what I'd been talking about the most. Things people have done or said that are fucked up, ways people have let me down, failures, bad behavior, rudeness, lies. The shortcut to human connection is meeting on the common ground of hating a third person. But that shit is low vibrational and leaves a fart fog of shittiness in the air. And sometimes, people already have so much shittiness going on in their lives, they just can't take another moment of it. Remember that.

Save the shitstorm for every fifth visit. Practice bringing something else to the table. If people ask you about a problem, try out the phrase, "It's so crazy, I don't want to get into it. What's good with you?" Then if they have to know something, they'll insist you tell them, but usually people are relieved.

This is the part where I, as your teacher, wheel out one of those old-fashioned overhead projectors and write on a piece of plastic with a dry-erase marker so it fills up the whole wall: EVERYONE NEEDS TO GO TO THERAPY. Because the burnout rate for friends listening to you go on and on about that one guy who you think likes you but you still can't tell and *ooh* what if he does but then *ahh* what if he doesn't is very, VERY high. As are you, for thinking anyone wants to sit in silence while you recount tales of the mild yet encouraging eye contact the two of you made at the office potluck. Get out of here with that jazz.

Please know I'm not judging you. Everyone does this. I certainly did it. OK, fine, I'll tell you about it. Once upon a time, I fell in crush with a douchebag. During this dark time, I could not stop talking about him. It was constant and mind-numbingly dull. I was also on diet pills, so it was truly the un-coolest phase of my life. I'd become a shaking, sleepless, fixated, but finally skinny weirdo. And I was convinced if I could just win this one specific heart, all my problems would disappear. My clutch friend Laura (note: not my *sister* Laura, who is also my clutch friend, but I'd never call her that because she'd make fun of me) had been with me through all of it and often took the brunt of my new, awful, drug-addled personality. She'd also done speed when she was in her twenties, so she was especially understanding and forgiving— until this one day. While she drove us to lunch, I started in again on my monologue about where he might be and who he might be talking to, and finally, my very nice and patient friend lost it. I'll never forget it. She slammed on the brakes right in the middle of Beechwood Canyon and screamed, "STOP TALKING ABOUT HIM! IT'S NOT REAL! IT'S NOT HAPPENING! HE DOESN'T LIKE YOU! LET IT GO!" It cut right through my drug-deafness and self-obsession. I finally saw myself from the outside. It was horrible, and it was the nicest thing anyone had ever done for me. I'd become a drooling, pathetic lunatic for a guy who clearly had no interest, but was probably bored and liked being adored, so he'd come sniffing around every four to eight months. And when he did, I'd talk about it for literally hours. People who don't care "yes, and" you. They'll help you stir that soup of sadness you're making because it somehow feeds them, too.

Have you always felt unseen, ignored, and unloved? Congratulations! You're the perfect prey for narcissists who feed off of blind worship and internal sadness. You'll never convince the target of your obsession that your love is what Sade was singing about on that one album. But oh, you will try. And in doing so, you will damage your self-esteem. And then, once you wake up from the stupid spell you put on yourself, you can rail against those narcissists, but it won't affect them. So it's better just to skip ahead to the part where you admit that you're the one who bought the ticket to their show. Choose to want to figure out why you do these things and how to stop. In the end, it's all you can do.

The people who do care about you will scream, "Shut up!" at you. Hopefully in a car or a private home. But however you get that message delivered: Take it. Ingest it. Heed it. And don't kill the messenger. Whatever form the message takes, it's always the same message at heart: get a professional to help you figure out why you do it. It's important.

A similar thing happened with my sister during the same dark time. We were on the phone, and I was telling her about the Douche and how he'd shown up at a party to find me and all these people were telling me, "Jerry was here. He's looking for you." And I was, of course, over the moon. When I was done telling her my amazing news, my sister simply said, "He sounds like a dork." Everything stopped.

A dork, she said. Suddenly, the voice in my head was being contradicted by a stronger, more reliable source—my older sister. I had to consider it. And when I did, the burden of obsession lifted for a second, and I could see the situation in a whole new way. Maybe instead of being rejected by a living god, I was actually narrowly escaping the grasp of some needy loser. There was a very good chance that, in truth, I was too cool for a dork like him. The novelty of this idea made me laugh uncontrollably. It was such a relief. I loved it, and I loved her for saying it. She hung up on me.

She didn't "yes, and" me. Of course she didn't. What older sister ever does? That's probably why I hadn't ever confided in her about this guy before. I knew she wouldn't go along with my melodrama. That's why my sister is my oldest and clutchest friend. She knows the real me, the me who my brain tries to convince isn't smart or pretty or good. She hears my bullshit and calls it out, "Shut up, Karen's brain. Get Real Karen back here now." And then it does. And then I'm there.

Now maybe you're thinking, *Well, I don't have an older sister or any clutch friends. Now what do I do?* Make some. It's not so hard. You just have to be interested in someone other than yourself. When people sit down to have a conversation, all they're looking for is something they can agree on or participate in with you. If you spend ten minutes complaining about your child's new preschool teacher to your single, childless friend, their interest will wane after thirty-five seconds. Resentment starts at two minutes, and it only gets uglier from there. Unless the preschool teacher is a famous criminal or circus escapee.

It's like those people who reference other people by their first name in a story but you don't know that person, so now you feel left out and rejected by your friend and this "René," who throws the wildest dinner parties. It's like they've written René into your two-person scene, but he doesn't have anything to do with your shared story. "This is René's favorite kind of tea. We went to San Diego and he drank it the whole time." *So what the fuck do I care?* is the common inner response. And after you turn forty-five, it's your outer verbal response, too. It's so fun when you start to feel the power of honesty. And if you can get to a healthy enough place where you wield this power in a responsible way, you'll become the clutch friend that people will someday reference in their advice book. That's the goal.

Don't treat your friends like they're the audience of your one-woman show. These are people who are good to you. Offer to them something high-vibrational. Think to yourself, *What's the most exciting thing I can say to this person?* For me, it's *Guess who likes you?* I hear that, and you have my full attention. In the fleeting moment between that question being asked and hearing the answer, anything is possible. It's pure, personalized hope. But that's not the case for my happily married friends. They have some other version of it. Try to figure out what that area of interest is for those around you so you can bring this level of joy to your friends whenever you can. And if you can't deliver them exciting compliments, tell them about how scientists have just discovered some new archaeological wonder. Because they always do and it's always good news for everybody. Hey! They just discovered humans have been working with bronze for fifty thousand years longer than previously believed. Fuck yes! High five! And did you know they found ANOTHER cave with even more Dead Sea scrolls inside it? Yes! It's true! How about those pyramids off the coast of Japan that some scientists believe to be proof of the lost civilization of Mu?! Wonderful. Go humanity! We rule.

And now, to wrap up this lesson, I'm going to take off my corduroy blazer, hop up on my desk, loosen my tie, and speak in low tones to tell you the worst best thing I know: all of this stuff gets easier the older you get because life just keeps getting harder and harder.

Shit happens out of the blue. Cancer, car accidents, someone you never believed wouldn't be there is just gone. It fells you. It empties you entirely. But eventually, as you grieve and heal, you slowly refill. You get real specific about what you need and what actually feels good. You refine your choices to avoid causing your own pain. But pain comes anyway. You start to see that it's supposed to. Adversity forces you to grow past reactive fear and self-preservation and into a worthwhile human being. Tragedy paradoxically begins to strengthen your heart. It breaks it, but then re-forms it as a better, stronger machine. And then you start to instinctually care about others. And you start to see how to be.

Friendship leads to human connection, which feeds your soul. More than kale or spinning or fifteen-minute naps under your desk, conscious communication with your clutch friends is the best form of self-care. It boosts your self-esteem. It makes you feel worthwhile. It gets your mind off your mind.

That is, unless you're a congenital, uncurable dickhead. Those people just blame, blame, blame until everyone leaves and the lights go out.

Class dismissed.

A Fun List of Tangible Items for Immediate Self-Care

I just told you self-care is about your friends, but if you're going to spend money on yourself to try to feel good, spend your money on:

- well-made shoes, purses, and jeans
- therapy
- cozy socks
- fancy lotion to slather all over your feet at night
- scented candles that smell like your grandma or that piano teacher you loved so much
- a good mattress
- health insurance
- a talented hairdresser
- hydrating face masks
- concert and theater tickets
- one nice piece of jewelry, like a watch or diamond-like studs
- good fruit
- pedicures
- a piece of art
- a donation to your local grammar school to pay for school lunches
- a subscription to *National Geographic*

Georgia Gets Her Nipple Pierced for All the Right Reasons

*Sometimes you just have to jump out the window
and grow wings on the way down.*
—RAY BRADBURY

The border between liberal, diverse Los Angeles County and conservative, WASPy Orange County is known by haters as "the Orange Curtain." I, my friends, am one of those haters. Every reality show you've seen depicting Orange County as a playground for upper-class narcissists with fake tans who actually use the word *bling* in everyday life is 100 percent true.

As a weirdo kid who fit in to none of those Orange County stereotypes, I felt the stifling weight of that curtain as soon as I was old enough to understand I could leave someday. And while it took me until I was eighteen years old to physically escape Orange County, I was lucky enough to find my way out via my imagination through books right in the nick of time. OK, I know that sounds super cheesy and woo-woo and all Mr. Rogers of me, but I really do think it's a miracle that I got out instead of ending up a drug addict or a lonely, bored housewife with a fake tan and tons of "bling."

When I was thirteen years old, I turned from a quiet, goofy kid into a straight-up, made-for-TV-movie-style juvenile delinquent. One minute I was a nerdy, self-esteem-less girl who wanted nothing more than to fit in with those preppy girls with starter credit cards but couldn't hide her natural weirdness (I wore socks with sandals and had a perm) and hyperactive goofiness (later to be revealed as ADHD), and by the time my thirteen birthday candles were giving off smoke and my bat mitzvah party was winding down, I'd pulled a one-eighty and ran screaming headfirst into my newfound life as the kid my friends' parents refused to let their daughters hang out with.

It all started with a cigarette. My older brother, Asher, had taken one from a party for me 'cause I wanted to try one. Not that it was my first cigarette. I'd crafted my own "artisanal" cigarettes out of loose tea leaves rolled up in a joint I'd fashioned from a paper towel and smoked in front of my bedroom mirror after school when I had the house to myself (shout-out to the latchkey kids!). If necessity is the mother of invention, then rebellion is her cool aunt.

I was so sure I looked super sophisticated and sexy as the plumes of smoke curled from my mouth and the ash and smoldering tea leaves dropped in flurries and singed my bare legs. In the mirror, I saw myself as none other than Audrey Hepburn with her awesome long-ass cigarette holder. Classy AF.

So *technically*, I smoked my first *real* cigarette with Asher out behind the apartments where he lived with our dad, directly across the street from where I lived with our mom and sister. That day, I learned that smoking actually means inhaling smoke into your lungs (cue coughing fit), not just into your mouth, and also that I had an insatiable curiosity for the more nefarious actions in life.

Over the next two years, smoking cigarettes both real and tea-filled turned to smoking pot, which turned to smoking meth, which was surprisingly easy to find in the '90s in Orange County. I shed my elementary school friends despite the fact that they were kind, smart people who would grow up to become tenured professors and marine biologists and other respectable things, and instead took to hanging out with the kids around town who were up to no good. My new friends came from broken homes like mine, where custody battles were the norm despite neither parent seeming very interested in actually parenting anyone. The dudes were older and shaved their hair into mohawks and played in (what I now realize were terrible) punk bands.

Here's a brief but exciting list of things that happened in my life when I was thirteen:

- I touched a penis for the first time.
- I stole money from the popular girls' backpacks.
- I tried meth.
- I started doing meth regularly.
- I stopped eating.
- I kept doing meth.
- I went to rehab.
- My grandmother died.

Obviously thirteen was a banner year for me.

Looking back, I feel so sad for the sweet baby angel I was. I couldn't see it at the time, but the anger that was fueling my rebellion was a badly worn mask attempting to cover a deep sadness and loneliness that started when my parents divorced. It's almost embarrassing to me how transparent it is now, but the staying out all night, the angry punk rock music, and the parade of crushes and boyfriends who were three-plus years older than I was were all part of a loud, obvious cry for attention.

How to Spot What Is Really Fueling Your Actions!

LOOK:

Take a quick inventory of your current life. Make a list of the very best things going on, like your cats, friends, loved ones you can count on (and your therapist, too!), a car that runs, nice feet, and so on. How would your life benefit from whatever actions you're taking or thinking about taking? How could your life be negatively affected by those actions if they don't turn out the way you planned? If you're reluctant to take this first step, chances are you already know your actions are being fueled by negative bullshit.

LISTEN:

Ask your cats, friends, and loved ones you can count on (and your therapist!), the ones who don't have a stake in your decisions, their opinion, and now here's the hard part: ACTUALLY LISTEN TO THEM! If you find that you're countering every single one of their thoughts with "Yeah, but . . ." or "I know you're right, but what if . . . ," then it's time to reevaluate your actions.

Deep down, I didn't think I deserved a normal, happy life like everyone else who fit in so well, so I actively tried to have an unhappy, abnormal one as a "fuck you" to that picture-perfect normalcy that so alluded me. I thought I was too stupid for school (again: undiagnosed ADHD), so I didn't go very often, which left me confused and behind when I did go, inadvertently proving my point. I thought I was hideously ugly, so I covered my face with copious amounts of goth makeup and wore grungy, torn clothing. If I could prove I knew that I was ugly by acting the part, then no one else would feel the need to tease me about it anymore.

To this day, I'm shocked I was able to get off that path before it left any lasting marks. Well, other than a couple of old piercing scars. And also, the at-home stick-and-poke tattoo of my then best friend's initials on my ankle, a design that's now covered by a pretty, professional tattoo.

Aside from those outward acts of rebellion—which are endearing in an eye-roll-inducing, crazy-stories-to-tell-at-parties kind of way—even at thirteen, I was self-aware enough to know that the meth and the eating disorder were not endearing. Even though my anxiety causes many negative issues, it also makes me hypervigilant to my behaviors, destructive and otherwise.

That anxiety was fueling me when, before school one morning, I pulled my sister aside and confided in her that I was worried my eating disorder was getting out of hand. I asked her to tell our mom for me knowing I couldn't face her myself, but I knew my sister, who was mature beyond her years, would help me.

Later that afternoon, before my mom had time to react to the news that her daughter was regularly sticking her finger into her throat to puke, I got caught doing meth at school. I'd just snorted up in my junior high bathroom (GEORGIA, WTF?) when the security guard caught me and brought me to the principal's office. My mom was given an ultimatum: take me directly to rehab, or I'd be arrested. Off to rehab I went!

I spent two weeks that included my fourteenth birthday there, and about one year to the day after my bat mitzvah, I was sent home. As I walked out the door for the last time, one of the nurses looked at me and said flatly, "You'll be back."

But post-rehab, I did go back to using, this time determined not to get caught. But after a couple of months, I quit on my own, cold turkey, after reading a book. Again, I know that's cheesy, but oh my god, I seriously love reading. And the book that was the catalyst for my salvation was . . . (drumroll, please) . . . *The 7 Habits of Highly Effective Teens*!

No, I'm kidding. It was *The Martian Chronicles* by Ray Bradbury.

Reading has always been important to me (I bet we have that in common, reader), thanks to my mom and her own lifelong love of reading, so I've been an avid reader ever since I was a tiny person. I'd sit in the closet underneath the staircase of my childhood home (like Harry Potter, but before there was a Harry Potter), atop a pile of afghans knitted by my grandma, with my cat, Whiskers, curled up in my lap. That was my favorite place to get the fuck out of Orange County and live somewhere else, even if it was only in my head. Sometimes I was convinced that when I opened the door back up to leave the closet, the real world would be gone and instead I'd find myself crawling into a fantasy world. I mean, shit, for all I know, maybe I did walk out into a parallel universe a couple of times.

> *The magic is only in what books say, how they stitched the patches of the universe together into one garment for us.*
>
> —RAY BRADBURY, *Fahrenheit 451*

On one of the days I actually showed up for class, my eighth-grade English teacher, who'd either been scared of me, or more likely *for* me, slipped me a copy of *The Martian Chronicles.* It was an older, worn copy that she must have brought from home. On the cover were two sleek Martians sitting amid an alien world and gazing at a star streaming across the horizon. My mind took me there, to that place on the cover. When she handed me the book, she said, "I think you'll like this." I started reading it under the stairs that afternoon. She was right. I loved it.

How could you not love something that starts like this:

The Men of Earth came to Mars. They came because they were afraid or unafraid, because they were happy or unhappy, because they felt like Pilgrims or did not feel like Pilgrims. There was a reason for each man. They were leaving bad wives or bad towns; they were coming to find something or leave something or get something, to dig up something or bury something or leave something alone.

The book is about humanity's experiences on Mars and the drive to conquer the planet. "We Earth Men have a talent for ruining big, beautiful things."

It's creepy and funny and scary and thrilling, and the prose is poetic and beautiful. My old copy is falling apart, and its pages are worn from reading and rereading, and you can still see the faint highlights from when I found a line or passage especially significant (those are the quotes throughout this chapter).

Reading one of Bradbury's books feels like watching an episode of *The Twilight Zone,* except instead of just inactively flopped on the couch, he makes you feel like you're living it. Like he'd written about spacemen and Martians and rocket ships specifically to drag me out of a dark closet into the sky.

> *All you had to do was pull a book from the shelf and open it and suddenly the darkness was not so dark anymore.*
>
> —**RAY BRADBURY,** *Farewell Summer*

He made me realize that the world was so much more than the suffocating suburbia I was growing up in, where I was an outcast because being "normal," which seemed to come so easily to other kids, was impossible for me. No matter how hard I had tried to fit in, I was always exposed as "weird."

And for the first time, I looked into my future and saw that my unhappy childhood was just the beginning. That things would be different later and that not being normal wasn't a bad thing, it was an asset, because nothing normal ever happened in his books.

> *The first thing you learn in life is you're a fool. The last thing you*
> *learn in life is you're the same fool.*
> —RAY BRADBURY, *Dandelion Wine*

I'd always been taught—at home, at school, in the media—that I was supposed to want college, marriage, babies, and a job in an office or a life as a housewife. All of that stuff can be amazing for the right people, but to me it all sounded like fucking bullshit, even as a kid, and not desiring those things made me feel like I'd failed as a person. Reading about other paths and unexpected journeys gave me hope.

I stopped hating my life for what it was and what it had been so far and started getting excited about what was going to be. I was excited about my future for the first time in my life.

I know it sounds crazy and far-fetched that *The Martian Chronicles* had such a profound effect on me, but that book came into my life at the perfect time. I'd continued to do drugs because I was bored, because life as a loser teenager was boring and my suburban-as-fuck town was boring and being me was difficult and boring.

This book opened up a whole new way of thinking that was So. Not. Boring. And it made staying in to read in my dusty nook under the stairs all night instead of going out to party with vapid friends and gross older dudes an obvious choice. I'd dabbled in juvenile delinquency, and I'm not going to lie, it was pretty fun while it lasted, but it wore out its welcome right as it was making me feel more trapped than free.

When I'd finish one of Bradbury's books—*The Martian Chronicles, Fahrenheit 451, Dandelion Wine*—I'd tear the paperback cover off and thumbtack it to my bedroom wall. Eventually, I'd read every single book he'd published, and then reread them. And he changed my life.

> *Time looks like snow dropping silently into a black room or it looked like a silent film in an ancient theater, 100 billion faces falling like those New Year balloons, down and down into nothing.*
> —RAY BRADBURY, *The Martian Chronicles*

So three years later, I was sixteen and I'd gotten my shit together. I stopped tattooing myself at home and skipping school, I discovered thrift stores and vintage dresses, and I'd limited my recreational inhaling back to the occasional nonartisanal cigarette. At some point that year, I found out Ray Bradbury was going to speak at the UCLA book fair, and my heart was like, *You have to go thank him.*

I had another incredible, caring English teacher at that time, Mrs. Mercer, and she helped me craft a long, thoughtful letter to give to Mr. Bradbury. I told him how much his work meant to me, and that I was so ridiculously grateful to him, and that I cherished his books. She also told me that if I wanted to get access to talk to Mr. Bradbury directly, I should wear something cute and to smile a lot and show off my dimples.

Now look, I know it's not very feminist to tell a high school girl that an influential older man will only talk to her if she looks cute, but I trusted Mrs. Mercer. She knew how to wield her femininity with confidence and power. She's one of the staunchest feminists I've ever known, so I listened to her when it came to advice on how to beat the patriarchy at its own game, despite it being somewhat antiquated.

I wore my favorite vintage dress, a lime-green day dress with giant daisies made by an old-school designer called Lanz Originals. Still my favorite vintage label. I stole my sister's favorite vintage '70s wedges and piled on my raver jewelry because it was the '90s and oh my god we had the worst fashion sense of any decade. (See: JNCO jeans, butterfly hair clips, hip-hugger jeans, tongue piercings.)

Even though I didn't have a driver's license yet, my mom knew how important this trip was to me, and she knew that I wanted to take it alone, so she let me take her car, and I drove stick shift in wedges the full forty-five minutes to UCLA. I had my window rolled down and I rocked my Deee-Lite cassette the entire way. To this day, it remains the most exhilarating drive of my life.

But it was my first time driving alone and my first time at UCLA, so I got lost, and by the time I found my way and parked, I was late to the lecture hall (later on, you'll learn about how much I love being late). Ray Bradbury's lecture was just about to start, and the theater was at capacity by the time I got there, so I was turned away by the college boy manning the door. In a fit of brilliant deception that came straight from the tiny rebellious thirteen-year-old me wearing devil horns on my left shoulder, I told my first of two lies that day.

Me, smiling sweetly: "Excuse me? Umm, my mom is inside, and I just needed to grab something from her purse really quick."

I flashed my dimples, watched the college boy clock them, and I was in! It worked! I strode into the auditorium with purpose and ducked into the only open seat right as *the* Ray Bradbury came on stage.

As he spoke, I tried not to barf from excitement or cry from admiration. I don't remember a single word he said, but when the lecture was over and the auditorium cleared out, I made my way to the stage, where he was being interviewed by a gaggle of male reporters.

I was so nervous, gripping my letter in my sweaty hand. I was sure I looked like a stalker and was going to get kicked out by security, but when there was a break in the questions from the reporters, I pushed past them and awkwardly thrust my letter at Ray Bradbury without saying a word.

"What's your name?" he asked as I stood staring, gobsmacked.

"Georgia," I stammered.

"That's my granddaughter's name," he said with a sparkle in his eye.

I blurted out that I was a huge fan and thanked him profusely. Then I turned around, vintage dress flouncing around my knees, and walked out of the auditorium. I swear to god I remember feeling like I was floating in my sister's wedges, excitement and nervous sweat radiating off me. He was also the first famous person I had met, so it just felt overwhelmingly bananas.

The day had gone so perfectly, and when I got back to my car, I just wasn't ready to drive back home and have it end. I needed a memento, something that would help me remember this day and how perfect it was. So with another idea whispered in my ear by the thirteen-year-old me on my shoulder, I headed off to Melrose Avenue and stopped at the first seedy tattoo parlor I could find. Then I told my second lie of the day.

Me, wielding my dimples again: "Hi, I'm eighteen and want to get my nipple pierced, but I don't have ID. Can you do it anyway?"

This lie worked, too, but I think it had more to do with the dude wanting to see my teenaged boob than with me being a cunning and believable liar or looking anywhere close to eighteen.

I got my nipple pierced, it hurt like a motherfucker, and then I drove home, giddy and exhausted. My best friend snapped this photo when I got to her house to tell her the story and show off my new jewelry.

Two weeks later, I got a package in the mail. Getting a package in the mail when you're sixteen is already the fucking best, but when I realized the sender was none other than Ray Bradbury, I nearly lost my mind. Inside the small box was a sweet note thanking me for my letter along with a copy of his book *Zen in the Art of Writing*, which he'd autographed and inscribed with what immediately became my favorite word and remains so to this day: *Onward!*

There's a great line from the book, which I also read and reread and still go back and read from time to time:

> *You must stay drunk on writing so reality cannot destroy you.*
> —**RAY FUCKING BRADBURY,** *Zen in the Art of Writing*

Since I'd first started reading his books, I had a secret wish to be a writer someday, which I told him in my letter. It wasn't something I, in my infinite lack of self-esteem, was sure I was smart enough to achieve, but here was a book about writing written by the master, inscribed with permission to move forward in this direction. I've been told it's basically the same as a degree in English. To be fair, I told me that. In the mirror. But I'm still banking on it being true.

I'm so relieved that my English teacher who thought I'd like *The Martian Chronicles* was right, instead of the nurse who insisted I'd be back in rehab.

And I'm so thankful to Ray Bradbury for giving the sweet baby angel that I was a reason to believe her life could be more. And it is. It's even better than I could have imagined.

> *We are cups, constantly and quietly being filled. The trick is,*
> *knowing how to tip ourselves over and let the beautiful stuff out.*
>
> —RAY BRADBURY

Sweet Baby Angel: Final Thoughts

GEORGIA: Do you think there's a sweet baby angel inside everyone?
KAREN: Yes, it's tucked up inside of your gastrointestinal system, right near the gallbladder.

GEORGIA: Do you think *you're* a sweet baby angel?
KAREN: Now I'm mad at you.

GEORGIA: Who's the biggest sweet baby angel that you know?
KAREN: Paul Giamatti.

YOU'RE IN A **CULT**

CALL YOUR

DAD

art by Rachel Ross

3

YOU'RE IN A CULT, CALL YOUR DAD

GEORGIA: This is Karen's quote based off my long-held belief that you should always have people in your life that will call you on your bullshit—like, for example, when you've joined a cult. But they'll also then offer to help you get out of said cult, even if they think you were dumb for joining the cult to begin with. And likewise, you should be there for your friends and family when they make dumb mistakes.

Karen on How to Not Drink the Kool-Aid
Even When You're Spiritually Parched

Wanna know what it's really like to live in Hollywood? OK, I'll tell you. I think you deserve to know the truth.

Most movies or TV shows set in LA start with the same five B-roll shots: Grauman's Chinese Theatre, the beach, Rodeo Drive, the Hollywood sign, and Channing Tatum waving from the red carpet. It's sparkly and opulent and so alluring. You see it and you want it. Your dreams are just as valid as Channing Tatum's, right? (Wrong, actually. That man is a powerhouse of talent and charm. Have you seen him in a cable-knit sweater? Holy shit, it's a religious experience.) So you pack up your dreams and move here like a hip, arty Dorothy heading to a sexy version of Oz. But then you arrive to find it's a five-hundred-square-mile parking lot filled with plastic surgery and parties you're not invited to. Then you begin to realize pretty much everyone is some sort of model. And the air is brown. And the traffic is insane. And so, disillusion sets in almost immediately. You hustle and schmooze, only to find to your great shock that no one in Hollywood cares that you were voted "Most Theatrical" in high school. Meanwhile, you constantly hear stories about younger, hotter, and less talented people being given cool jobs and piles of money. You begin to wonder why you ever believed in yourself. You start to feel lost, desperate, hopeless. It's the perfect environment for cult indoctrination.

I'm saying *you* here, but obviously I mean *me*. That was how it felt when I moved from San Francisco to Los Angeles at the ripe old age of twenty-four. I'd been living in the Bay Area for two years, trying to break into the stand-up scene and working at the Gap. It was a dark time that I filled with beer and burritos. About a year in, I became friends with the one and only Margaret Cho, who was living part-time in LA. She'd been really supportive and complimentary of my comedy from the day I met her. After about a year, she told me to send my tape to her agent. Her agent called me and said, "Move down here. I can get you work." And so I did. That's how I made big decisions back then. Does someone think I should do something? OK, I will. Does someone else think I shouldn't do that same thing? Fuck them, I'll do it twice. Wait, how do I feel about doing that thing? That's neither here nor there. It's what others think about what I'm doing that matters most. So even though I wasn't thin or beautiful or trained or connected and even though I only believed in myself as much as whoever was standing in front of me believed in me, I went ahead and moved down to Hollywood, into a big apartment building on the corner of Franklin and Fuller Avenues. And soon I would learn that just 1.8 miles down Franklin Avenue was a huge, gothic mansion shrouded in trees and surrounded by iron gates. The sign on the front gate read, "The Celebrity Centre."

I became fascinated with Scientology after moving to LA. The church had been expanding rapidly, and everyone I met was freaking out about it. I didn't know much about any of it, except for those ten-second commercials for Dianetics I'd seen on TV as a kid, but I'd assumed they were for some sort of bizarre science fiction thing. Turned out, I was right.

I met people in LA who had stories about friends joining Scientology to help their careers and getting sucked in. They'd lost all of their money, they'd cut themselves off from everyone they knew. If they tried to leave, they were stalked or sued or slandered. Not exactly standard "church" stuff. It was so scary and dark and bizarre, I was positive I was going to join at any moment. It just seemed like something I would do.

Because that's the thing about cults: they make it real easy to join. They try to convince you they have the Answer. They try to appeal to your deepest needs. I mean, who doesn't want to hang out in a place called the Celebrity Centre? It sounds like, if you could just get inside, Jack Nicholson would be there to greet you with a huge smile and a cigar. Welcome, you've made it in Hollywood. Your worries are over. Here's the bad news: your worries are never over. They just keep coming. Eventually, you have to learn how to deal with them yourself. There is no one answer. It just isn't simple.

And anyone who tries to convince you otherwise has an agenda. Maybe I should've written that first (do we still have that projector?). EVERYONE HAS AN AGENDA. No matter who it is: your aunt, the government, raccoons. We're all just out here in the world trying to get what we want. You are, too. It's not necessarily a bad thing. It's also not permanent. You can change your agenda at any time. Just don't let anyone convince you to put your agenda aside in place of theirs, even if they claim to have all the answers. *Especially* if they claim to have all the answers. *Ugh.* People who claim to have all the answers NEVER have ANY answers. Anyway, thanks for buying this advice book.

When I first started going to my therapist, she'd sit there in her midcentury chair with her cup of tea listening to me ranting endlessly on her moss-green sofa about all the people I hated or who I was afraid hated me. I had so many problems with so many people. It made me feel like a monster.

After about two months of listening to one story after another about betrayal and heartache, she asked, "Have I ever told you the thing about your inner circle?"

I took a breath, slightly irritated that my monologue was being interrupted. "No."

"How many close friends would you say you have?"

"Ummm . . . like thirty? Or so?"

She looked surprised. "Oh, no! No, that's too many."

"Really?"

She smiled, nodding. "Five."

"Five?" I recoiled.

"I'm talking about real friends. Most people have one to five. Any more is too many. The inner circle needs to be small. You can still have all your acquaintances. They belong in the outer circle. You don't go to them with important stuff because they don't know you well enough. Then there's the next circle in, casual friends. They're closer than the outer group, but they're not close enough to be inner. The inner circle are your best friends. The ones who will drive you to the airport. Those are the relationships you should be putting all of this energy into."

I stared at her, feeling that life truth resonate around the room.

She smiled again. "That's all the time we have."

To some people, that might all be obvious, but it blew my mind. I'd been operating under some weird leftover high school drive to be popular. Popularity is a numbers game. I never thought about the quality of those relationships at all. I was bringing inner-circle problems to people who were really in the outer circle, then complaining when it didn't go well. This is where the idea of the clutch-five friend came from, it's become one of my most valuable and useful beliefs.

And that's the thing about therapists—they never claim to have all the answers, but they actually do. And they're being paid to not have an agenda. And to help you with your agenda. And to watch you cry. They're the inner-circle model to help you recognize what inner-circle behavior should look like. Then it's just about identifying your inner circle and bringing them in close.

It's no coincidence that one of the first things cults do is cut you off from your friends and family. That's because we're all more apt to accept nonsensical bullshit and terrible treatment if there's no one standing next to us making the "you've gotta be kidding me" face. Don't believe anyone who tells you the people who love you are bad for you. That's a huge red flag. No one who wants the best for you wants you to have *less* human connection. That's strictly villain shit right there.

We're all crazy and scared and searching. No one gets to use that against you. It's not proof you're broken, it's proof you're human. If you can get used to being wrong, saying you're sorry, and staying open to possibilities, you won't feel so panicked when things don't go according to plan. And the less you panic, the less you'll feel the need to find someone with the Answer. Figure out who you are, what you stand for, and who you love. Put them in your inner circle. Make sure they're smart and strong and that they love you. Be a good friend to them so they stick by you. That way, when life gives you lemons and you lose your shit and join a cult, you'll always have a "dad" you can call.

There are tens of thousands of people living in Los Angeles who moved here because they thought they had what it takes to become famous actors. But only about nine people ever really do. So over time, this city has become densely populated with once-hot citizens critically wounded by their own broken dreams. It's like a battlefield in the Civil War, I imagine. All these people desperately staggering around Hollywood with open psychic wounds, silently screaming for a medic.

And they keep on trying for years on end, auditioning over and over, only to be told, "No, thanks," or worse and, more commonly, nothing at all. That's the ugliest part of the Hollywood system—when you don't succeed, there's no "Nice try; here's what you could've done better." You simply never hear back. Showbiz ghosts you. So you end up obsessing over every stupid role like it was your young lover taken on the battlefield before his time. Except no Ken Burns–narrated letter ever arrives telling you that you must go on living and how beautiful you looked in the morning light while a sad fiddle plays in the background. There is no bad news, only darker and darker shades of denial.

It's fun at first. You leave your audition actually believing you did such a good job that you will undoubtedly be cast as the surly cashier in the film *What Women Want.* They loved you. You nailed it. You tell several (twenty-two) friends that you essentially have the part. You tell them it's essentially the best script you've ever read. You watch them burn with jealousy. You make a mental note that that kind of toxicity is bad for you. You start a list of people you need to cut out of your life after the red carpet premiere. You practice smiling and waving for said premiere. This goes on for roughly two days. All the while, you're checking and rechecking your phone. Always nothing. On day three, your conviction begins to fade. You retitle that friendship cut list "People I May Have to Borrow Money From." On day four, you begin blurting out, "No news is good news!" to anyone you see on the street. You decide it's best to stay indoors so when the good news comes, you'll be in familiar surroundings. You go home and wait by the window, pretending not to feel your hope slowly fizzle out. And then . . . day five hits. You wake up early, knowing whatever hope you had was internally manufactured and entirely ridiculous. You're not getting that part. They did not love you at all. You feel pathetic and unsure of your own perception. You're wounded and lost in the wilderness of Hollywood, your compass is cracked, and your self-esteem is developing a serious case of gangrene.

Five years inside that cycle of hope and rejection renders you a quaking shell of your former self. This is why cults of every variety do so great down here. Fake sci-fi religions, plastic surgery, improv classes—there are all kinds of belief systems to escape into. This town has a snake oil salesman on every corner, promising to provide you with the one and only cure you'll ever need. And you need a cure so bad that you're willing to try just about anything.

Here are the two most destructive ones I've joined:

The Cult of Booze

I devoted myself to this belief system as a teen, right when bottled wine coolers were getting popular, and I stayed in until I was twenty-seven. I LOVED drinking. I loved it like a first crush. I got all hot-faced and excited when I knew I was going to get to drink. Beer, wine coolers, random liquor shots from our parents' liquor cabinet. It felt dangerous and glamorous and like it could make something happen. I held on to this erroneous belief until the day I was hospitalized with seizures. The doctor told me they were probably from alcohol withdrawal. I argued that I'd never stopped drinking. The doctor stared at me, bewildered. He asked how many drinks I had a night, on average. I did some quick math: I usually only drink after work ends, say from 10:00 P.M. to 1:00 A.M., and I probably had four drinks an hour, which would mean I had twelve drinks a night on average, but that sounded like too many. I knew it'd be bad to tell him I was consistently putting up double digits, so I lied and said, "Eight."

He rolled his eyes. "No, not how many drinks *a week,* how many a *night*?"

I tried to smile. "Eight."

The color drained from his face. "Eight? A night?! Good lord."

"But so does everybody else I know!" I whined.

He wasn't listening. He was busy writing mean, judgmental things about me and my social life in my chart. God, I hated that guy.

The problem with my thinking was that even though all my friends did drink as much as I did none of them were in the hospital for grand mal seizures. Just me. All alone. Trying to explain my rad social life to this high and mighty pilgrim doctor. Oh, I'm sorry, Pa Ingalls! Are you scared of partying? Is that why you always got your homework done and became a doctor like a little bitch?

In hindsight, I see that this mind-set was wrong. A dozen drinks a night is about nine too many. Three or four is right in the pocket for a good night out. Anything above that and you're likely to come to an hour later in the middle of your starring role in the whisper/scream/barf show.

I know it can be fun, but also, you're drunk, so how would you know? Eight beers in and what's actually fun versus the interpretation of a brain drowning in liquor are hard to discern. And if you truly believe you need that many drinks a night to have fun, you are mishandling your needs. You definitely must have as much fun as you can in this life. But is making out with a mailbox actually fun? Yes, it might break federal law, which is a hoot. And lightly debasing yourself with a dusty inanimate object to make your friends laugh can be wonderful, sure. But is it mental-scrapbook-of-good-memories fun? Naw, baby. It's just a royal-blue blur in the mental slideshow of "What the fuck did I do last night?" You need to get enough of those good, clean fun times going in your life so you have something to weigh that drunk fun against. It's good to learn the difference and be honest about how your behavior makes you feel.

Here's an example:

I have a beautiful, singular memory from my late twenties (post-drinking) of swimming in the ocean with my friends. It's one of those memories I escape to when I'm sad or panicking, as it's immediately relaxing and joyful. It's just six of us, all out past the breakers, that Everclear song–style, treading water and talking and laughing and floating together under a summer sky. Everyone was overtly happy, and everyone looked great wet. I'd just lost a bunch of weight after I stopped drinking, so being in a bathing suit in public was a huge victory for me. Things finally felt like they were going to be OK. At one point, someone tried to put someone else on their shoulders while treading water and yelled, "Chicken fight!" We all laughed, but then another guy and his wife tried to do it, too. We started arguing about the pros and cons of having chicken fights in the middle of the ocean. I yelled that our being out there was dangerous enough, but as I said it, I realized it wasn't true. I wasn't scared one bit. There were so many of us together, I knew nothing could happen to us. As stupid as that might sound, for that one moment, it was actually true.

We need our brains to be clear and healthy at least part of the time so we can notice and record these tiny, magical moments in our lives. A drunk brain can't do that—it's myopic, hard of hearing, and on a constant five-second delay. And because alcohol is a depressant, it rarely picks up on the tiny, powerful goodness around you. That's just not how it interprets reality. The cult of booze tries to brainwash you into thinking you need it to have any fun at all, when the truth is exactly the opposite. If you're not careful, it will kill all the fun entirely.

The Cult of Perfect

I grew up in the '80s, right when supermodels got popular. Suddenly, people like Naomi Campbell and Linda Evangelista weren't just amazing anonymous faces in fashion magazines, they were major celebrities. They popped up in music videos and movies and talk shows. They were extremely gorgeous and dangerously thin. They were always laughing through their big white teeth or glaring like they just missed the bus. They wore tube dresses with combat boots and everyone still got a boner. They could have haircuts that looked like a white-wine drunk went at them with safety scissors and it would become the new trend. They looked good squatting. They had it all.

Suddenly, it wasn't enough to be cute anymore. You had to be striking and starving. I watched this trend explode with a white-hot panic. There was no way I could compete. My butt was huge. My hips were wide. I had freckles and a big face and a space between my two front teeth. But it got worse. In sixth grade, I developed deep, red stretch marks on my inner thighs. They were disgusting and mysterious, showing up one morning out of the blue as if I'd been attacked by a panther in the night. Then I started noticing broken blood vessels behind my knees just like my grandma at the pool. My legs were so pale they looked grayish blue, so every vein and hair follicle showed. I knew I could never wear shorts or a miniskirt with no tights ever again. I was too disgusting. Finally, I had to face it: I DID NOT HAVE WHAT IT TOOK TO WALK THE RUNWAY IN MILAN, and it genuinely broke my heart. And it made me *hate* myself.

I began to keep a mental list of all the things I needed to get fixed so I could one day at least be pretty. It was simple. I just needed to have my butt, thighs, and stomach surgically removed. While I was under for that, I'd ask them to throw in a quick nose job and implant some huge white teeth. I also needed full-body electrolysis, leg-extending surgery, a year-round tan, finger-fat liposuction, nail-bed enhancements, large-pore ensmallments, and of course, shy lessons.

From age thirteen on, there was never something I didn't loathe about me; always something to notice, wince at, cover, and then burn with shame about. I envied the popular girls at my school, and I dreamed of somehow becoming the prettiest of them all. That desire filled my head with insane, desperate ideas. If I could just stop eating for five minutes, maybe I could figure out how to be anorexic like a model. But deep down, I knew I was already too big for that to work, which would fill me with anxiety, which I would soothe with food. I was watching the beauty boat slowly pull out of port as I stood alone on the dock of permanent invisibility. I couldn't believe it! For a while there, I really thought I had something to offer. But there was no middle ground. If I couldn't be Cindy Crawford, I was nothing.

The cult of perfect, deep down, is just fear. We want human connection, but we're psychotically afraid of rejection, so our head tells us to stay home until we're good enough. But when you get older, you learn the shittiest, most ironic life lesson: "perfection" is not a guarantee for happiness. This was never clearer to me than back when I read the shocking news that Sandra Bullock's husband cheated on her. What?! How? Sandy is America's sweetheart. She's gorgeous, down to earth, legitimately funny, and genuinely talented. Her husband looked like some guy you'd see at the hot dog stand outside of Costco. And yet HE cheated on HER?? This was when my stranglehold on the dream of perfection began to loosen. So I'm supposed to suffer and sacrifice and put someone else's demands of me before my own happiness and I'm STILL going to get my heart broken? What the fuck?

Well, it turns out life is not a meritocracy. If you show up, even in the most perfect human form, you will get your heart broken. You just will. That's part of the deal. No one gets out unscathed, unless they stay home. But then you just get scathed in a different way. (Is *scathed* a word by itself? If it is, I like it. It sounds like it burns.) You get scathed with loneliness.

We run around making ourselves miserable and insane trying to be the Best One, when we should really be aiming to become Our True Selves. That's how you can deprogram yourself out of this cult. Know your failures, while being painful and horrifying now, will be great stories you can laugh about in ten to fifteen years. Your imperfections aren't a reason to hide. They're actually the key to connecting with all the other imperfect humans around you. I stole all of this from my therapist, Michelle of the Midcentury Furniture. She's been telling me this for as long as I've known her. I used to think she was full of shit, but the older I get, the more I'm willing to believe it's true.

Georgia on Kleptomania and Calling Your Dad

When I was thirteen years old, I went through an awkward phase and a kleptomania phase at the same time. Most people keep those phases separate, but . . . (leans chair back, puts hands behind head) . . . I've always been an overachiever.

I'd gotten this amazing jean jacket as a Hanukkah present from my grandma that I loved so much I practically wore it in the shower. It was really just a basic Levi's jean jacket, light wash, sleeves rolled up, collar popped. It was way too big for my tiny frame (did I mention I was also going through a starving-myself phase? Yeah, I was basically triple majoring in being a fuckup). The best part was that the jacket had these two deep pockets hidden on the inside that were ideal for hiding the loot I'd steal.

I started stealing around the same time I smoked my first cigarette. Almost overnight, puberty had changed me from a sweet, bookish girl who was eager to please and impress adults like my mom and my teachers to an adolescent misfit who wanted nothing more than to earn the title Problem Child. It's the usual worn-out trope of "I'm not getting the attention I so desperately crave by being good, but hey, look! When I act out, I have all the attention in the world!" Super misguided, yes, but it worked.

I went from sneaking into my mom's bed to cuddle in the middle of the night and spraying my pillow with her perfume when I went to sleepaway camp 'cause I missed her so much to getting in screaming, crying, tantrum-level fights with her before school every morning because I wanted to stay home and watch *The Price Is Right* and eat cheese toast all day.

Like smoking cigarettes, stealing stuff felt like an excellent way to rebel and show the world I was no longer that timid girl they thought they knew. Ultimately, I think I really just had such vastly low self-esteem that my desire to be someone, anyone, else found an easy home as a rebel. Plus, being a juvenile delinquent turned out to be super fun to boot! Pleasing everyone and trying to fit in and be normal had proven to not just be exhausting but impossible since at my very core I'm not really the fitting-in type. Hardstarks are weirdos at heart, but I didn't learn to appreciate that weirdness until much later.

The other bonus of stealing was that I was finally able to have the things I thought I was owed. The stuff we couldn't afford on my single mother's salary and child support from my dad which seemed like obvious basics to most kids. I had always known that my family was one of the few in my school that were broke, and I think I had become pissed off about it. Going to the grocery store meant bouncing a check 'cause my mom didn't have the funds in her bank account, but we needed food. Hand-me-downs from various cousins (mostly boys) filled out my wardrobe, a wardrobe I caught shit for every day at school. I saw my poor mom cry over too many bills, and asking for anything—badly needed new underwear or a bra for my budding tits—was met with fretting over how we could afford it. When I discovered stealing, I found a way to provide for myself. I was angry, and I felt like the world owed me something for my years of going without. I was now providing for myself in abundance-ville.

OK, now back to my accomplice, the jean jacket. I knew that the usual way of stealing by slipping something into your purse or pocket was too obvious and a sure way to get caught. Instead, I took advantage of those two giant, hidden inner pockets that were begging to be used for nefarious business.

Item in hand, I'd casually, slowly, imperceptibly slide my hand up inside the large sleeve of the jacket and drop the goods into the inside pocket, then slide my hand back out through the sleeve. To the naked eye, it didn't even appear that I had moved my arm at all. Genius, right?

An Incomplete List of the Very Important and Necessary Things I Stole Using My Accomplice, the Jacket

- my first pair of G-string underwear
- a cassette of *Blood Sugar Sex Magik* by Red Hot Chili Peppers
- a set of tarot cards that I was then told was cursed for having been stolen so I promptly gave it away
- a bottle of knockoff CK One perfume from the local swap meet
- a bunch of Stussy and Ocean Pacific stickers from a surfer/skater store to put on my school binder
- fancy shampoo and conditioner from a beauty shop
- so many boxes of Marlboro Red cigarettes from Target
- countless pieces of makeup from Target
- the dignity of the security guard who my BFF and I outran at Target

The day I got caught shoplifting for the first time was the day I stopped. My best friend, Meg, was my accomplice in my budding rebellious phase, along with that jacket. We had become friends the year before when we were on the same soccer team, and we'd quickly become inseparable. She was a super-smart tomboy and she had a natural athleticism. Having a strict father meant that her rebellious phase didn't go beyond sneaking an occasional cigarette and stealing a cheap bottle of nail polish a couple of times. In the not-too-distant future from the day in question, her parents would forbid her from being my friend anymore, not wrongly determining that I was a bad influence. We'd take very different paths in life and lose touch as soon as I started spiraling into a drug habit and skipping school, while she excelled academically and grew up to become a tenured professor. But back at thirteen years old when the playing field was more even, she was my best friend.

Our local mall was a huge high-end beast of a thing called South Coast Plaza, where trophy wives shopped and lunched on weekdays and where I had been coming since I was a baby to ride the gorgeous antique carousel. Meg and I were popping into our favorite (aka easy-to-steal-from) retailers, on the hunt for the preteen klepto trifecta: distracted shopgirls, easy-to-pocket items, and lots of other shoppers for us to blend in with.

We found the perfect target that day in Charlotte Russe, a cheap, trendy eyesore of a shop that blasted R&B and sold slutty clubwear. I zeroed in on a cute pair of earrings that I was much more interested in stealing than I was in wearing. I think they were gold hoops? But honestly, I don't remember. The point was never the thing I was taking, if that makes any sense. The point was that I wanted something and I wanted *even more* to fulfill that want, hoping maybe it would fill that bottomless pit that was my lack of self-esteem. Maybe these earrings would be the thing that finally made me cool enough.

The SECOND I dropped those cute but not-even-really-worth-owning earrings into my trusty secret inner jacket pocket, something was off. I just knew it. This woman was weirdly close, trailing me as I tried to act all casual and look like I was just browsing (picture a gawky, guilty kid in the throes of puberty and you can imagine how nonchalant I *didn't* look). I grabbed Meg by the arm, whispering, "Go, go, go," and pushing her out the door like I was some kind of flat-chested James Bond with (neon bands on my) braces.

Meg got out first. I didn't make it. The moment I passed the threshold from store to mall, a firm hand landed on my shoulder. It was the woman from the jewelry aisle. I had heard about "secret shoppers," but I'd never spotted one in the wild. I guess that's the point.

She led me back into the store. Meg stood frozen with fear in the freedom of the mall. I was in big fucking trouble. We both knew it. I tried to say, "Goodbye forever," with my face, and she responded with "I will tell your story" eyes before turning to find a pay phone to call her sister to pick her up.

The secret shopper led me back through the crime scene into a small, windowless office in the bowels of the store. I was directed to an uncomfortable folding chair beside an ugly beige tanker desk, where I was ignored by my captor and a very pregnant employee sitting behind the desk. They discussed me as if I wasn't there.

Nodding at her colleague's belly, then me, Secret Shopper asked, "You ready to have one of these?"

Super Pregnant gave me one look. "God, I hope it's a boy!"

They laughed it up, and I slouched heavily and symbolically into my trusty jacket, wishing I could shrink down small enough to disappear inside the inner pockets myself, from shame as much as fear of what was to come. Something so much worse than prison. The phone call to a parent.

A vision of my mother and her clenched-teeth anger turned my blood to ice. If I called my mom, I'd get a spanking. Even the *thought* was humiliating. I was thirteen—*thirteen*—and still getting *spanked.* I'd gotten my period! I smoked cigarettes! I was a fucking grown-up (in my mind, only)! I wasn't the little girl that got punished with slaps on the butt anymore, and I guess I was hoping that my rebellious antics would have shown her I was a worthy adversary and, fuck, maybe even make her a little scared of me. Scared enough to not be totally sure how I'd react if she tried to hit me again.

So instead, I called my dad. My parents were seven years into their totally-not-amicable divorce (more on that later), and while my mom ruled with an iron fist and a wooden spoon, my dad had a much harder time controlling me, Asher, and my sister, Leah. We got away with *a lot*.

My dad had custody of us every other weekend, and when he'd inevitably exhausted all the options for entertaining three rambunctious kids (there was a lot of miniature golf and free museums in my childhood), the weekend would turn to the last-resort childhood babysitter, a rented movie. As this was the '80s / early '90s, any nonbasic electronic equipment was solely owned by rich people. Luckily for our electronics-deficient family, the tiny mom-and-pop video store nearby rented out VCRs along with their movies for the weekend.

The thing I remember most fondly about this place is the small, red velvet curtained–off section in the back that held the most interesting thing in the world: pornographic videos.

The porn room was, of course, totally off-limits to children. I imagined a world of sexy sex stuff that I wouldn't understand until I was a grown-up. Being so intrigued by the idea of porn and sex and grown-up body parts, I convinced myself that this room held the answers to the weird questions I had about fornication, such as how on earth people had sex without crushing each other and what on earth a penis looked like. Anyway, I'm going somewhere with all this. We'll get back to me at the slutty clubwear store in a minute.

So one fateful Saturday-night video store trip, as my siblings and I were fighting about what to rent and Asher was throwing a tantrum at my dad in another aisle because he lost out with his choice of *Top Gun* to my and Leah's choice of *Dirty Dancing* for the hundredth time, I saw our opportunity. I glanced over at my sister, and in unison, we turned and bolted down the aisle, and with a swish of the red velvet curtain, we were in. We'd entered the coveted porn section.

I was turning in circles trying to take in the four walls of graphic video covers before we got caught, but it was too much! I couldn't focus on anything! In an uncharacteristic burst of self-control, I re-member forcing myself to stop and stare at just one cover so I could commit it to memory. To this day, I can perfectly recall the picture on the box and the name of the movie.

A cute, pert coed with huge back-combed '80s hair and a big smile stared back at me from the cover. She was proudly displaying her al-most complete nakedness, but the focus of the cover was her giant scrunched white socks and her petite white Keds. The video was called *Naked with Shoes On.* My mind was thoroughly blown.

Of course, we were caught in a matter of seconds by my dad and the store clerk, but our only punishment was Leah and I got our *Dirty Dancing* privileges revoked that night, though as we sat and watched *Top Gun* (boring), I'd never been more pleased with myself. Naked! With shoes ON!

So yeah, back in that cramped clothing store office as I held the receiver in my hand (shout-out to the readers who know what a dial tone is!), there was no question.

I also knew that my parents' dislike of each other was at an all-time high (more on that later), so I knew my dad wouldn't tell my mom, but that didn't mean I was out of the emotional-punishment woods (more on that right now). Because here's the thing—my dad has the worst of all disappointed-dad reactions: he's a crier. He's the kind of guy who takes on all my bad behavior as his own fault. Have you ever seen your dad cry because of something you did? Girl, it will break you.

But being broken is better than being spanked, so I made the call, and my dad dropped everything to come bail me out.

He cried, I cried, Secret Shopper and Super Pregnant did not cry. I apologized for being an asshole. Weeks later, a bill came in the mail for whatever charges get applied when a kid gets caught stealing some dumb earrings (stolen item's price + security charges + penalty for be-ing an asshole). My dad wrote the security company explaining that my assholeness was due to my behavioral issues stemming from depression and anxiety and the charges and fees should really be dismissed, please. And clearly that wasn't a lie. If stealing at thirteen years old isn't indicative of behavioral issues, then I don't know what the fuck is.

No matter how deep into shit you get, there will always be someone who is willing to help you, if you just reach out. Whenever I read about the Jonestown massacre (which I do a lot, 'cause it's fucking fascinating) my heart breaks. Over nine hundred people, some purposely, some forcefully, drank poison because their cult leader, Jim Jones, commanded them to.

I've always wondered where that point of no return was for those members. Probably way before the cyanide and moving to a commune and turning over all worldly possessions. What was the moment that they didn't think there was an out anymore? Didn't think that someone in their life, outside the cult, would be there to help them if they reached out? And it makes me think of my family, because no matter how fraught my relationship with my mom or sister, or what modest means my dad would be able to provide to help me get back on my feet, not having a ton of worldly possessions himself, I know they would always be there for me if I reached out. It makes me sad that hundreds of those members had family who would have done anything to help them but that at some point they decided it wasn't possible anymore to make a call.

For years following the shoplifting incident, my dad would swoop in many more times to help me with even worse trouble. Drugs and boys and huge fights with my mom. Luckily, I eventually straightened out, but even in my twenties, I could call him to ask adulting questions like, "How do you apply for a credit card?" and "What is a résumé supposed to look like?" He helped me open my first bank account and made sure that the moment I got my driver's license, I had AAA, just in case. The other thing he does is always, without fail, tell me how proud he is of me whenever we part ways, either in person or on the phone. Even when I didn't deserve anyone being proud of me, he still made sure that I knew that he was proud of the person I was, even when that person made (lots of) mistakes.

Fun fact: the shoplifting charges were dismissed! And to this day, my dad hasn't told my mom about it. But I guess I kind of just did. Sorry, Mom.

You're in a Cult, Call Your Dad: Final Thoughts

GEORGIA: When was the last time you had to ask your dad for help and thought, *Whoa, I'm way too old to be asking my dad for help*?

KAREN: It was about five years ago when I had to borrow money from my dad because I couldn't pay my mortgage. I'd been pretending the financial problems I was having didn't exist, which I absolutely do not recommend. Denial usually triples the size of any problem. Not only was I way too old to be running to Daddy's checkbook, I was too old not to see that it was a very short-term Band-Aid. Like one of those off-brand Band-Aids that comes off an hour after you put it on because you bend your thumb wrong. You know the kind.

GEORGIA: What's something you wouldn't know how to do if your dad hadn't taught you?

KAREN: Let's see: tell a good story, make beef stroganoff, drive a stick shift, appreciate classical music, insult people creatively, sing, make good popcorn.

GEORGIA: Out of all the cults in history, which one do you think you would have been most likely to join?

KAREN: Is the Illuminati considered a cult? They've always seemed appealing to me because they're so secretive. I don't even know who or what they are, yet I'm kind of afraid to be talking about them in print. That's power. It's just kind of understood that they run shit, but they keep a tight lid on things. They're not making commercials inviting you to join. You CAN'T join. They don't want you. That's the only kind of group I've ever cared about.

GEORGIA: If you were to start a cult, what would the rules be? Could I join?

KAREN: My cult would be like one long game night you're not allowed to leave: charades, Yahtzee, gin rummy, Risk, all of it. Just constant hanging out and playing games and eating onion dip. The leader of the cult will be determined by who wins the most games that day, so it'll end up rotating, thus preventing extremism. Oh, and everyone has to have a black bob. Georgia, I hate to tell you this, but you're already in it.

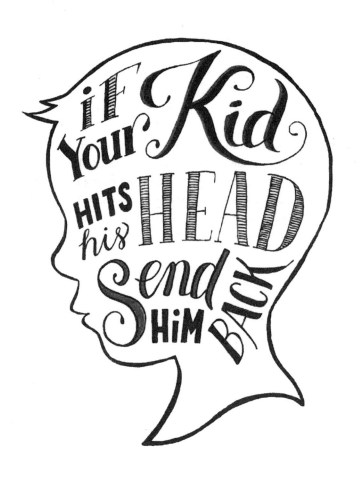

iF Your Kid HITS his HEAD send HiM BACK

art by Rita Garza of RitaWorks Art & Illustration

4

SEND 'EM BACK

KAREN: The one realization Georgia and I have come to as we read story after story about murderers to each other is that almost every serial killer suffered a major head trauma as a child. They all got hit in the head by a swing. Or kicked in the head by a horse. Or a third thing. And afterward, things in their brain went haywire. So Georgia, child-rearing expert that she is, suggested that if your kid gets kicked in the head, you should probably "send 'em back." Who knew that in this age of helicopter parenting this idea would strike such a chord? Turns out, lots of us have been hit in the head as children and lots more have accidentally hit their children in the head. We're all afraid to find out which one of us will turn out to be the bad apple. That's why it's important to learn about and look for red flags in all children, especially ones who were forced to raise themselves on horror movies and powdered lemonade.

Georgia on Car Crashes and Meeting Karen

I blame Stephen King for my addiction to fear. It all started when I was just ten years old. I was a skinny kid with stringy hair, an overactive imagination, and an obsessive, all-encompassing love of books, cats, and snacks . . . so basically, I was the exact same person I am today. I loved nothing more than getting cozy with a paperback from the local library in the grandiose-sounding neighborhood of Heritage Park. Maybe a Roald Dahl or a Judy Blume, with Whiskers curled up at my feet and a plate of cheese toast and apple slices beside me.

But I also loved scary movies, like any good anxiety-ridden person does, despite the insomnia that accompanies them. Back in the '80s, adults didn't bat an eye at a kid watching terrifying movies that would give them nightmares for months. We watched movies about stuff like a dying murderer using black magic to possess a little boy's favorite doll (*Child's Play*), and a baby who gets kidnapped by a goblin king and the baby's big sister who has to survive a big creepy maze, grotesque Muppets, and David Bowie's junk-hugging leggings to get him back (*Labyrinth*). My mom recently reminded me that for my eighth birthday party, a sleepover, she rented us little girls the gory and graphic *Robocop*, featuring violent cyborgs, and left us to watch it in the dark alone. Parents had to be called for pickups within the first twenty minutes of the movie.

Our baby boomer parents, who as children had duck-and-cover drills during class due to legit LOOMING NUCLEAR WARFARE, must not have thought fiction was that big of a deal.

I think kids are way too sheltered these days and some exposure to the real world is necessary for growth . . . that said, there's some shit I saw as a kid, both fictional and non-, that greatly contributed to my pretty significant anxiety disorder. So yeah, maybe don't let your kid watch *Robocop* at eight years old (I'm side-eyeing you, Mom).

And even though I'd heard scary stories late at night at sleepovers, nothing prepared my ten-year-old ass for the terror that was *Pet Sematary*. How did I have the opportunity to watch horror when I was ten? Well, my parents divorced when I was five, so they weren't around after school due to their work schedules, and they weren't around at night due to their dating schedules, so as latchkey kids, what my siblings and I watched on TV was not policed.

"Georgia, what's a latchkey kid?" you ask. Excellent question! You see, way back before helicopter parenting, a kid was allowed to be home alone for hours on end with no supervision while their parents were at work or at a bar or wherever (also cell phones didn't exist yet, remember?). The latchkey part comes from the house key that was either on a string around the kid's neck or hidden in an obviously fake rock in the garden. During their parent-free hours, latchkey kids were expected to just hang out at home or go out into the world and live their fucking lives or whatever, all without supervision. We're all still shocked that the majority of us weren't kidnapped or killed.

If it sounds like fun, stick around for Karen's step-by-step guide next!

So there we were, under the supervision of our regal gray-and-white alley turned lap cat, settling in on our very '70s tacky brown plaid couch under a couple Grandma-knitted afghans for a night of that exhilaratingly awful-yet-wonderful feeling of being terrified by a movie. If you've never seen *Pet Sematary*, go watch it. Right now . . .

. . . Fucking terrifying, right???

To be fair, it's corny and hokey, as most early Stephen King movies are, but that's part of the charm. It knocked a neuron or two loose in my ten-year-old brain, and I still haven't recovered. I was *so* that little girl who would rather see her beloved cat become a smelly, evil zombie-cat than have no beloved cat at all. After that movie, I became fascinated by the concept of terror and gore, and so thanks to Stephen King, I became addicted to the feeling of fear. I needed more.

I started checking out Stephen King books from the Heritage Park Library, consuming the thick paperbacks at a rate that would've worried my parents if they weren't so busy working and dating. I started with *Pet Sematary*, which turned out to be WAY scarier than the movie, then moved on to some of my favorites like *Christine, It, The Dead Zone,* and *The Shining.* Each one kept me up reading late into the night.

I've always had anxiety-induced insomnia, which causes me to lie awake and stare into the darkness, thinking about all the worst things that can befall me and those I cared about. These books were teaching me about new and awful befall-able things, but now I had Stephen King keeping me company, so I wasn't alone anymore. Any insomniac will tell you that it's not as bad when you have someone to share it with.

Within a year or two, I'd read through the library's entire Stephen King collection, but my love of scaring the shit out of myself late into the night had only just begun.

And somewhere along the way, I got my hands on something even scarier, the biography of a serial killer. Not just any serial killer. Ted Freaking Bundy. And not just any biography. *The Stranger Beside Me* by the goddess that is Ann Rule. Stephen King and his fictional fear were a gateway drug to the hard stuff, the real-life terror of true crime.

I was horrified. And thrilled. And I wouldn't know it until the term was coined twenty-six years later in the *My Favorite Murder* Facebook community page, but I became a Murderino.

I was lucky no one in my family ever shamed me for my fascination with true crime. In fact, they were in it with me. At the time, *Unsolved Mysteries* and *America's Most Wanted* were two of the biggest shows on TV, and the faces of missing children were plastered on the milk cartons that sat on our breakfast tables. Thinking back, I don't know how anyone else who grew up when I did *didn't* become obsessed with true crime. The '80s practically forced it down our throats in the name of TV ratings. There isn't one person my age who doesn't still get the chills when they hear the gravelly, soothing voice of Robert Stack or hear the creepy theme song from *Unsolved Mysteries.* But while everyone else in my generation seemed to outgrow their fascination with true crime, I fell deeper in love.

I didn't know it was something I was supposed to be embarrassed about until I got a little older and realized that people thought I was a creep for wanting to talk about murder all the time. Apparently, it's creepy to obsess about the weapons most commonly used in familicide, the analysis of bloodstain patterns, and the psychological profiles of people with Munchausen syndrome by proxy and to want—no, have to—know all the tragic, horrible details, and yes, even see crime scene photos and read autopsy reports. And did I mention my waking nightmares of being kidnapped? But I couldn't quit.

Much in the same way I loved being terrified by Stephen King, I loved how Ann Rule made me feel that my constant anxiety about death was legitimate. Look, there it was, right on the page! Georgeann Hawkins had been worried about a Spanish test instead of the very real threat of someone lurking in the shadows, and then that someone manifested into Ted Bundy and snatched her off the street. It was real! I wasn't crazy!

Anxiety had been a very real, very problematic part of my life long before I stumbled upon true crime. I was already lying awake in bed at night, paralyzed with fear: worry that something awful would happen to my parents or my siblings or my cat, worry about the future, about being made fun of at school, about car accidents and what-ifs . . . those things kept me up at night already, true crime or not.

There was something so satisfying about getting confirmation that the world wasn't as great as *Happy Days* or *Mr. Belvedere* made it out to be. It didn't take the anxiety away, but it still felt like a fucking triumph. I was a child, and I wanted to know about every bad thing that's out there so I could prepare myself for the worst, and what the hell is worse than a child murderer?? Literally nothing. Not. One. Thing. I didn't just want to feel the thrill of fear or the satisfaction of validation, my survival *depended* on my knowing about crime.

Ann Rule even says in *The Stranger Beside Me* that her ultimate goal was "to warn women of danger, and hopefully save their lives with some bit of advice or caution they read in my books." I was determined to glean as much of that advice and caution as humanly possible. I was going to arm myself with knowledge.

In fall of 1993, Polly Klaas, a girl my age on the other side of California, disappeared out of her home. She was abducted while surrounded by her friends at a slumber party, plucked from her sleeping bag and carried out past her mother's bedroom and into the cold night. It seemed like such a dirty trick to steal her from the safety of a room full of her best friends. I didn't know her, but I lay in bed at night imagining her escape from her captor, willing it to happen. I'd picture her untying knots with her teeth and wriggling out of restraints, running through a field to a lonely highway and flagging down a passing car who would carry her to safety.

Polly didn't escape. She was killed. When her captor was found, a story came out that Polly had been alive hidden in the nearby woods while a cop helped the sick fuck pull his stuck car from a ditch. I was so angry that I knew for sure that life wasn't fair and never would be. I knew that if sweet Polly wasn't safe from the dark ironies of life, then there was no way that I was either. I had always had a hunch about this aspect, but now I was sure.

But anxiety wasn't the only thing I carried out of my youth and into my adolescence. Along with the fear, there was a growing understanding that not everyone was in this with me.

When I got older and realized my peers weren't super into true crime like I was, I learned to suss out those who shared my passion by picking up on little hints like favorite TV shows (*Law & Order, CSI*, anything on Discovery ID), and later I figured out I could trick people into discussing true crime by asking my favorite conversation starter, "What's the craziest thing that happened in your hometown as a kid that fucked with your head?" I hung on every word of the real-life stories I was told, about kidnappings and murderers and teachers revealed to be child molesters. Everyone had a story, even if they purported to not be into true crime.

Enter Karen

I didn't just find a friend when I met Karen, I found a kindred spirit. We met through mutual friends, and although we'd been at a couple of parties together, we hadn't really talked much. Over a decade earlier, when I was twenty-one, I used to see her perform at this tiny restaurant turned comedy venue called Largo. Karen was so cool and funny, and I was uncharacteristically intimidated by her the first few times I met her.

But at a Halloween party in 2015, before our convo about *The Staircase* and before our first lunch date which turned into an idea for a podcast which turned into this book which turned into a similar story in the intro to this book, but from her perspective, I heard her from across the room talking to a small gathered crowd about a gory car accident she'd witnessed the day before. I needed to know more. So as everyone around her slowly backed away to find a conversation that involved less blood, I moved in closer, grabbed her by the arm, and with grave sincerity said, "Tell me everything."

Car accidents are another of my big anxiety triggers. When I was sixteen, my first "real" boyfriend, a sweet redheaded boy named Mike who I'd met at summer camp a few years earlier, was killed when the car he was driving got swept up in a flash flood and ended up under the wheels of a big rig. I found out about Mike's death when my sister called me at my high school boyfriend's house. We were broken up at that point—me and Mike—but it still fucking wrecked me.

And then there was high school boyfriend Chris. I'd met Chris during my two-week stint in rehab. We were in for the same drug of choice, meth, and a little while after rehab we both ditched the meth and fell madly in love. It was an obsessive relationship that was, while not quite healthy, an important one in terms of teaching me about relationships and love. We eventually broke up, and I graduated high school and moved away, but we kept in touch, and I always had a place in my heart for him.

A couple of years later, I got a call from Chris's older brother. Two nights earlier, Chris had driven off the freeway into a wall and had sat dying in his car for hours before being spotted the next morning. He was alive when he was pulled from the car but died on the way to the hospital. It took me years and lots of therapy to stop constantly picturing him waiting in his car for hours to be found. Was he conscious? Bleeding? Scared? The night he crashed, I'd suddenly woken up at 3:00 A.M. with a start and a piercing, painful headache. I eventually fell back to sleep, but later on I put it together that the moment I woke up, he was in his car dying from his head injury. I'd wondered for a long time if he'd been thinking about me at that moment, or if the synapses firing in his broken brain had briefly popped on to some memory of me that I could sense in my sleep. I'm not a superstitious or really even a spiritual person, but it just felt like there had to be some connection.

So cut back to that Halloween party, Karen in scrubs and me as Glenn Danzig. I begged her for the details of the accident she'd witnessed because I find it impossible to bury my head in the sand and pretend this kind of thing doesn't happen.

I could sense her passion for the macabre as she described the accident, and from there, our conversation transitioned easily into true-crime documentaries and cases that we were obsessed with. Any Murderino will tell you how exciting it is to find someone who can talk to you about murder without judgment or hesitation, and Karen and I found that in each other in that small Los Feliz kitchen, after everyone else walked away. I could tell she was just as stoked about it as I was.

We met for lunch a short time later at a semi-hipster café in Holly-wood and sat for hours after our tuna melts were finished, just drinking endless cups of black coffee and talking nonstop about our lives, our favorite cases, and mutual friends. We were giddy! Not just at having someone to talk to about true crime but at that thrilling feeling of making a new lifelong lady friend; that's harder and harder to come by the older you get. Maybe it's because we both happened to be reading Brené Brown's *Daring Greatly,* a book about being vulnerable, but both of us opened up to each other in ways I don't think either of us were used to.

Sometime the following week, I texted her and asked if she wanted to start a true-crime podcast, and she said she did. I don't think she knew yet that I'm the kind of person who's obsessed with starting new projects, because she seemed surprised when I responded to her with some options to schedule our first recording. As I've said on the pod-cast, it doesn't have to be perfect, just fucking do things. Perfection-ism is for people who are lying to themselves. The Cult of Perfect would not accept me as a member, which is just fucking fine with me. I'm a jump-into-the-deep-end-and-see-if-you-can-swim kinda girl.

We had a quick planning session over yet more tuna melts and came up with the format of each of us telling the other one murder every episode. Karen thought of the name *My Favorite Murder,* I told her about my fucked-up hometown-stories obsession and we decided to include it, and a couple of days later in January of 2016, we recorded our first episode. Within a couple of months, the podcast blew the fuck up, and my life completely changed in so many wonderful, amazing ways.

Even after all this time, I'm floored that I get to study and discuss a topic that has always fascinated me. I get asked a lot if my anxiety about murder has gotten worse since we started the podcast, since I have to hear about it so much (SO MUCH). But truthfully my anxiety has actually lessened based solely on the fact that the podcast has made me realize how many people there are in the world who are just like me. It makes me feel less alone every time I see our download numbers. I'm not a freak. I'm a Murderino, and I feel so stupidly lucky that I get to be a Murderino.

What was the chapter topic again? Oh yeah, send 'em back.

Whatever. Close enough.

On to the next project!

Karen's Step-by-Step Guide on How to Be a Latchkey Kid

For as much as Georgia and I have talked about what it was like to be latchkey kids growing up, there seems to be a large swath of our listenership who, either because they had stay-at-home moms or were born in the '90s, have no idea what we're talking about. Congratulations on being actively cared for when it matters most. Now sit down. I'm about to tell you exactly how to be a latchkey kid.

3:45–4:00 P.M.

Yell thanks to the carpool mom dropping you off as you jump out of her carpool car and follow your older sister, Laura, up the front walkway. Just to bug her, stand directly behind her as she gets out the front door key. Get close. Get real close. Feel the air get knocked out of you as she throws her elbow back and into your stomach. As you clutch your guts in pain, watch her walk into the house and slam and lock the door behind her.

Laugh yourself through the pain as you remember you have your own key. Pull the long string out from inside your school uniform. Unlock the door. Drop your book bag wherever. In the distance, your sister's bedroom door slams. Walk into the kitchen.

Feel hungry. Decide to make toast. Put bread in the toaster and wait.

Feel thirsty. Decide to make lemonade. Open the cabinet and pull down the can of lemonade powder. As you do, look at every single thing on every shelf like you've never seen any of it before, just in case your mom bought something new and delicious for you. She didn't.

Entertain the idea of making the box of spice-cake mix your mom's had in the cupboard since last Christmas. Put it into your mental "good ideas for later" file between "look for spare change in the couch" and "act shy at school." Pull out the Tupperware juice container and mix up some lemonade. As you stare into the plastic pitcher, wonder why your mother chose mustard yellow for her Tupperware set when avocado green is so much cooler. Put that question in your mental "questions to ask Mom when she gets home" file. Stop stirring. Put the lid on the lemonade pitcher.

Hear the toaster pop. Butter the toast. Feel a surge of love for the concept of toast. Get a napkin. Put away all ingredients. As you put the lid on the powdered lemonade, dip your finger into the tiny dune of yellow powder and then taste it. Feel a shiver of joy. It tastes just like candy! Eat more. Remember that you have toast waiting. Take your snack over to the couch. On the way, swing by the TV and turn it on with your elbow.

4:00–4:30 P.M.

Eat your toast while you lie all the way down flat on the couch watching cartoons. It's a *Scooby-Doo* with special celebrity guest Jerry Reed. Add "who is Jerry Reed" to the urgent section of the "questions to ask Mom" file. Try to take a sip of your lemonade while lying down. Spill lemonade out of the side of your mouth onto your face. Wonder if this is how it was for Cleopatra.

Oh! Remember you have new slippers! Run up the hallway as fast as you can. As you walk by your parents' room, remember you left your headband in there. Go in and get your headband off of your mom's nightstand. Look through your mom's nightstand drawer. Experience genuine disappointment when there's nothing salacious inside. Steal two quarters lying at the bottom of the drawer as a boring tax. See your slippers in your parents' bathroom. Put them on.

Run as fast as you can back down the hall and slide through the kitchen in your new slippers. As you run back up the hallway, see your sister's bedroom door fly open. She's smiling and wearing her slippers.

4:30–4:45 P.M.

Get super excited that Laura, who never participates in any of your great ideas, is finally going to try running slipper slides herself. Tell her she can go while you run out to the living room and turn on the radio. Take turns running down the hall and sliding through the kitchen for what feels like an hour. Get mad when your sister goes twice in a row because Rick Springfield came on so she said she had to slide to that song first since he's *her guy* and it's *her song.* Feel the burn of injustice as you remind her that she already said Matt Dillon was *her guy.* Watch her ignore you and slide anyway. Feel the burn ignite into a fiery rage. As she passes you, push her as hard as you can, mid-slide, onto the dining room floor.

Hear her fall loudly and then skid on her knees on the carpet.

Hold your breath and wait, trying to psychically sense how hard she will retaliate.

Feel your stomach drop as you hear her scream in pain, but then feel it ricochet back up as she begins laughing hysterically. Laugh harder as she calls you swears. *Who cares about swears?!* Watch her jump up and run over to the La-Z-Boy recliner. Get mad that you didn't think to sit there earlier. Remember you have toast waiting and get excited again.

4:45–5:45 P.M.

Keep eating toast while you watch cartoons until you begin to feel sick. Lie on the couch in every possible direction to relieve the pressure. Remind yourself to not eat that much toast tomorrow.

Look over and notice how cozy your sister looks in the La-Z-Boy recliner. Get mad again that you forgot that chair was yours for the taking, even though you're normally fourth in line when the rest of the family is home. Notice how she's not noticing you notice her. How come she can do that and you can't? Start a fight over the fact that she's been sitting in the La-Z-Boy recliner long enough and now it's your turn. Immediately lose the fight when she replies with the inarguable:

"Shut up, you baby."

Simmer with rage. Tell yourself you are definitely not a baby. Drink the rest of your lemonade exactly like a baby, all gulpy with both hands on the glass. Hear your sister call you a weirdo. Look over at your sister reclining in that big stuffed chair like she's the fucking king of Siam. Think of all the nice older sisters you know. Ask god why you got such a mean one. Hate her actively. Suddenly remember that you have lemonade powder waiting. Smile. Try to think of something to do that's better than sitting on a dumb chair. Hear the commercial for the game Operation start in the background. Jump up in front of the TV and recite every line of the commercial so perfectly it makes the king of Siam burst out laughing. VICTORY. Watch her laugh harder and harder, until she rolls out of the chair and onto the ground. Jump on her. Hear her cries for mercy as she screams, "I'm peeing!" Watch her crawl, still laughing, to the bathroom. Scream after her, "THE CHAIR IS MINE!"

Sit down in the La-Z-Boy recliner and recline so far back you begin to tip backward. Say, "Ahhhhh!" like you're a man in a beer commercial. *Oh!* Remember you have lemonade powder waiting! Listen for the sounds of how close your sister is to being done changing out of her pee pants to calculate how much time you have and if it's safe to risk getting up to get the lemonade powder.

Remember that the universe favors the bold.

Make a run for the lemonade powder can on the counter, sliding past it by about three feet.

Turn back to get it. See your sister speed-slide past you, through the kitchen. *Scream.* Don't stop screaming. Watch her jump in slow-motion over *your* chair arm and into *your* ultra-reclined recliner. Watch as she begins to cackle like the satanic beast that she is.

Hate her.

5:45–6:30 P.M.

Feel your internal rage thermometer skyrocket and explode out the top of its thermometer head, Daffy Duck–style. Change the atmosphere in the room with your mere feelings. Watch as your sister feels the barometric pressure drop and turns to look at you, fear creeping onto her face.

Stare back icily. Smile. Drop the can of lemonade powder back onto the counter loudly. Slowly turn and walk up the hallway to the bathroom. Open the bathroom drawer. Grab the closest hairbrush. Slam the drawer shut as a warning signal: the fun and games are over. Things are about to get scary.

Hold the brush up over your head and run as fast as you can back down the hallway, screaming like a banshee, and slide through the kitchen into the living room. Land at the La-Z-Boy and begin to beat your sister with the brush as hard and fast as you can.

Get clocked, hard, in the ear by her panicked, flailing arms. Squeeze your eyes shut in pain. Feel her grab the brush out of your hand. Watch as she throws her weight forward, kicking down the footrest and vaulting herself out of the La-Z-Boy recliner. Scramble away. Feel your feet slipping around beneath you in your new slippers, just like *Tom and Jerry*. Find your balance and take a step away.

Feel the yank on your hair as your sister grabs a handful and pulls you backward onto the ground. *Scream.* Scream as she straddles you, pins your arms under her knees, and beats *you* with the brush. *Scream for your life.* Try to say the neighbor's first names in your screams so someone will come over and save you. Get hit with the brush multiple times around the head and shoulder area. Stop screaming and say in your normal voice, "Ow, Laura!"

Watch her not stop. Become filled with the rage of a thousand lifetimes . . .

Make a frightening grunt sound.

Pull an arm free.

Slap her across the *face.*

Watch her reel backward. Buck her off you, scramble to the fireplace, and grab the poker. Watch her hold her face with hot tears in her eyes as she calls you a ton of swears and storms off to her room. Hear her door slam. Wait. Run and slide and grab the lemonade powder off the kitchen counter. Run and slide back into the living room and jump onto the recliner the way your sister did before.

See the poker on the ground. Realize you're going to need it to defend yourself for at least two more hours until your mom gets home. Lean over and grab the poker. Recline in the recliner for twenty-two delicious minutes of uninterrupted television viewing. Who's the king of Siam now? Make a mental note to ask Mom who the king of Siam is now. Don't file it away. Get it done tonight.

6:30–7:00 P.M.

Startle when your sister returns to the living room, giving your recliner a wide berth. Watch helplessly as she walks up and changes the channel.

Yell, "Hey! I was watching that!"

Watch as she stares you down from beside the TV, smiling like a demon. She says, "Come and change it, then."

Realize your sister has you trapped in a gilded cage of recliner occupation. Watch helplessly as she strolls over, grabs your glass of lemonade. Look away as she takes a huge swig. Feel a powerful thirst. You are a castaway on La-Z-Boy Island, and that's the last of your fresh water. Ask your sister to please give you the glass. Watch as she laughs in the scary way and takes another loud gulp of your lemonade. Say a swear at your sister. Flinch when she moves to hit you, then throw up the poker. Watch as she hits the poker instead of you and hurts her hand. Laugh hysterically, but do not pee. Stand your ground from your reclined position. Prepare to watch six more hours of TV.

7:00–7:30 P.M.

Look out the front window into the blackness of the night. Get a weird feeling. Put down the shade. Forget that you're fighting with your sister because *Three's Company* is so incredibly funny and, more importantly, dirty.

Listen to your sister ask you a question only a dumb person would ask. Tell her that and then say the answer. Hear her tell you to shut up. Hear her complain that there's nothing to eat. Tell her to make you both biscuits. Hear her say no, then make a noise like she just remembered something. Watch as she gets up and smiles sarcastically as she walks around you in the recliner. Know that she's planning some sort of retaliation. Feel your mind reel at the possibilities of what she could be planning. Engage your senses. Listen as she walks up the hallway to her bedroom. Hear the door close. Wonder nervously what she's doing. Know that it's time to give up the chair.

Tiptoe silently up the hall to her closed bedroom door and press your ear against it. Hear a distinctive crunching sound. Throw the door open and yell, "Aha!" *Scooby-Doo*-style. See your sister flinch as she lies on her bed eating from a box of Captain Crunch!! What. How.

Sugar cereal is second only to white drugs in things that are taboo in your family's home.

Slowly realize your sister has somehow acquired and is now hoarding breakfast contraband behind your back. Realize further the larger idea that your sister hides food in her room. *Scream.* Scream with an odd mix of jealousy and joy. Watch her lying frozen, mid-bite, staring at you. Decide to play the surprise element. Ask nicely if you can have some. Watch her clutch the box to her breast like a wild animal and scream, "Get out!" Know that you have several options as to how you'll get that box of cereal out of her hands. Begin to run scenarios. The smash-and-grab. The long con. The I'm Telling.

Feel a jolt of fear as you hear the doorbell ring.

7:38 P.M.

Watch your sister's eyes go wide. Turn and run down the hall. Hear your sister get up and run after you. Slide to the front door. Feel your sister's hand grab at your arm as she whispers:

"Don't open the door."

Open the door.

See a man standing on your porch. Get an odd chill realizing he's a stranger. Listen as he says he's dropping off firewood and asks if your parents are home. Go to answer. Feel a yank as your sister pulls you backward, steps in front of you, and begins speaking in a lower, smarter tone of voice.

"My mom has the flu so she's asleep right now, but my dad is right next door. He'll be back in one minute."

Watch as the man waves her off and hands her an envelope.

Watch her close the door, turn to you with her wide eyes, and raise a finger to her lips as if to say:

Wait. Be quiet.

Wait and be quiet.

Watch your sister's face as she listens to the man walk back up the front walkway. See her Navy SEAL hand signals as she silently tells you to follow her and tiptoes away. Kick off your slippers and follow her, also on tiptoes. Watch her duck down to peek out the kitchen window at him. See the man pause and turn back to stare at the house. Feel your stomach drop.

Duck down behind your sister and bury your head in her back, making a little scared sound. Feel her hand try to push you off her as she whispers, "Stop touching me!" Punch her in the butt for not letting you hide on her. Feel her hiss the word "Stop!" at you. Stop.

Watch as she belly crawls into the living room like an alligator. Follow like a crocodile. Mimic her as she slithers up onto the couch, staying below the bottom of the picture window.

Watch as she listens for him to pass that window and open the door to his truck. Feel how quiet it is. Wonder who the man is, what he wants, and how exactly he is going to kill you both. Wonder if the man has ever dealt with girls so well versed in fireplace-poker fighting. Wonder if the man has ever had anyone pin him down and spit in his ear. Feel the fear recede a bit as you convince yourself the two of you could take him and break him.

Hear the door of his truck open and the weight of the truck shift as he gets in.

Hear the engine start up and the truck back out onto the road and drive away.

Feel the fear recede further.

Follow your sister as she slowly sits up and lifts the window shade to make sure he's gone. See that he is gone. Watch as your sister turns and looks at you, half-scared, half-thrilled. Stare at her in frazzled silence. See her make a weird face that you can't read, then hear your sister fart. Laugh in surprise. Hear the fart continue. Realize that it is not a short toot, but the longest, trumpety-est, most air-filled fart you've ever heard. Laugh harder. Almost die. Stare in amazement as it continues. Begin to scream-laugh. Watch as she begins to laugh. Listen as her fart begins to poot out along with her laughter. Go insane. Laugh so hard you feel like you're going to stop breathing. Realize that nothing funnier has ever happened or will ever happen.

Continue to laugh for roughly three minutes after the fart ends. Fall back on the couch. Remember you made lemonade. Go to get some. Watch as your sister remembers she can take the recliner. Be glad to see it go. Walk back to the couch with your lemonade. Forget to leave a safety zone. Feel a jolt as your sister sticks her foot out to trip you. Catch yourself just in time to not fall or spill your lemonade. Scream bad swears at her. Watch her smile like the devil himself.

Sit down on the couch and spill the lemonade all over the front of your school uniform, which you are supposed to take off when you get home, but for some reason never do. Watch the lemonade pill up on the military-grade polyester plaid your uniform is made of. Pull the fancy blanket your mom lays on the back of the couch down and wipe the lemonade off.

Watch the cat walk into the room. Compete with your sister to see who can get it to come to them first. Win. Hear your sister say she hates that cat, anyway. Make eye contact with the cat as if to say, "What a sore loser." Snuggle with the cat. Look over at your sister, who looks very alone on her recliner. Think, *I've been there.*

7:50–8:10 P.M.

Think about your homework in a distant, wistful way. Watch *Entertainment Tonight* knowing your parents wouldn't want you to. Think about going into your sister's room and figuring out a way to steal her Captain Crunch. Feel the throbbing welt on your cheek and the bruises on both shins. Let that pain mix in with the TV show you're watching. Begin to hate Mary Hart.

Hate her.

See the long, white headlights of your mom's Volvo pan across the now-black picture window. Hear the garage door go up, the engine go off, and the garage door go back down. Feel a tightness in your throat and a dim longing as the door to the garage swings open and your mom walks in. Watch as she surveys the living room and kitchen, then stares at you and your sister, exhausted. Hear her give the same speech she gives every night around this time:

"All I asked you to do this morning was clean up the living room before I got home, and you didn't do it."

Flash back to her telling you over breakfast how helpful it would be if you and your sister could tidy up before she gets home from work. Realize it's the first time you've thought about that moment since it happened. Feel genuine shock at your selective amnesia.

Watch sadly as your mom walks into the kitchen and starts to pull out pots and pans to make dinner. Look over at your sister. Watch as she gives you a look of regret and shame. Follow her as she gets up and goes into the kitchen.

Hear her say, "Sorry, Mom."

Yell over her, "Sorry, Mommy!"

Hear her yell over you, "I love you, Mom!"

Yell louder, "I love you more, Mom!"

Watch as your mom turns toward the two of you, coat still on, holding the can of lemonade powder. "Was someone *eating* this?"

Freeze.

Wonder how she can know these things. Anticipate more yelling. Watch as she sees your guilty face and begins to laugh. "Jesus. What have you two been up to?"

Fun & Easy Latchkey Recipes!

Toast

    2 slices of Lombardi's sourdough bread or equivalent
    1 lb of butter

- Put two slices of toast in the toaster. Make sure it's not set to burnt. Push the thing down.
- Wait for the toast to pop back up. Do not stick a fork into the toaster at any point. Even if your toast gets stuck. This is important. Don't tell yourself you can do it because you're special. Just don't go down that road. It'll end in tears.
- Get a paper towel so you don't have to rinse a dish. Butter the toast on it. Really help yourself to that butter. Drown in it, rescue yourself, and then teach that butter a lesson about who's in charge.
- Repeat.

Lemonade

    1 can of lemonade powder
    Tap water

- To hell with what the can says. Put as many scoops of that good, young lemonade powder into your mom's Tupperware juice container as you see fit. Fill the rest up with tap water. Throw some ice cubes in if you're in a hurry.

Biscuits

2¼ cup of Bisquick

⅔ cup of milk

- That's it! Isn't that crazy? Two ingredients! Mix those two together and boom! You're halfway home.
- Preheat the oven for 10 minutes at 450 degrees. The oven is no game. Fear the oven. It will burn you. And it will burn your biscuits.
- Set a timer for 10 minutes for the preheat and then mix your dough. Glop it onto a cookie sheet and put that in the oven for 8–10 minutes.
- When you go to pull it back out, use two oven mitts and re-play in your mind that Thanksgiving when your mom scalded her forearm on a hot oven rack and then had an oven rack tattoo for the next thirty years.

Send 'Em Back: Final Thoughts

KAREN: As you know, Georgia, many of the serial killers we've talked about sustained serious head injuries when they were children. Tell us about any head injuries you sustained in childhood or anytime afterward.

GEORGIA: Thankfully, I never had any head injuries as a kid, at least that I can recall, but I did have one seizure when I was like twelve. It was while I was sleeping in my top bunk, and my sister had the bottom bunk. She heard and felt me seizing out and ran into my mom's room and yelled, "Mom, Georgia's having a cow!" We were really into *The Simpsons* at the time. I came to in the hospital and still regret that I was unconscious for my first and hopefully only ambulance ride.

KAREN: What's the thing—an event, a TV show, a friendship, anything—that you think fucked you up most as a kid?

GEORGIA: Oh, gosh, there are so many to choose from! On a personal level, the thing that really screwed me up was getting pantsed in the fifth grade in front of my entire class. I was in a fight with my then best friend, Kelly, and so during PE, she ran up behind me and yanked my skirt down around my ankles. I remember it vividly. It was like time stood still as I crouched down to pull my skirt back up while cowering to cover up my purple underpants. It seemed like it took forever to cover myself up, and all the kids were laughing hysterically at me. I really don't think I got over the humiliation until I was an adult.

KAREN: If you could return children like they were shoes from Zappos, how many would you get, and what would you name them?
GEORGIA: I wish this were possible because I'm so on the fence about having kids. I would just want one nerdy kid that loved books and being quiet and didn't need help with math homework. I'd name him Lewis, and he would be the sweetest kid.

dont be
a fucking
lunatic

art by Jenna Beddick

5

DON'T BE A FUCKING LUNATIC

KAREN: If you listen to the show, you know we're not shy when it comes to talking about our checkered pasts with substance abuse. Not only is it a cathartic form of shame-purging, but there's nothing like a humiliating drinking story to keep you grounded. We share these stories of glaring failure so that you can learn from our stupidity, save yourself some pain, and hopefully, be a little less of a lunatic.

Karen's Plan for
When the Party's Finally Over

Oh, sweet reader, of all the areas of life you will visit, this is one where I really know my stuff. I've thoroughly researched this topic vis-à-vis extensive field testing over roughly a thirty-five-year period. I've been being a lunatic for most of my life, just been being one all along, through and through. And although it's had its high points, overall I can't say it served me well. I taught myself at an early age that when things got scary, I had to run. So the second I got nervous or felt vulnerable, I filled the air with nervous blather, spent endless nights in crowded bars, repeatedly lied to myself that Long Island iced teas were the answer, cried freely while confessing my unrequited love to someone I didn't know that well, and on and on. Not a lot of championship moments in my yearbook.

But instead of falling into an indefinite trauma pocket about it, I figure I'll walk you through my life of DON'Ts in the hope that you can steer around the emotional sinkholes I've flung myself into. Being a lunatic can feel good in right-sized doses, as long as you know how deep the sinkhole goes and when to get back out.

How to Party

But first, a quick sidebar to all the unsupervised twelve-year-olds who got their hands on this book, thinking they're going to see pictures of dead bodies and read a list of swears: Get out of here, dummy! This isn't for your ears.

Oh, so you've decided to stay? OK, fine. But just know that by continuing to read, you've legally given up your right to sue if the entire concept of partying is ruined for you by the time you're done with this chapter.

The first thing that should be realized and accepted when it comes to partying: for every problem it "solves," it creates ten more. Yes, it's fun and cool, and crazy things happen, but the thing about escaping is, at some point, you have to come back. If you leave the studio apartment of yourself for too long, all the emotional plants die. I know that's a terrible metaphor. I'm still trying to get the twelve-year-olds to leave.

I was also going to say that partying doesn't make you popular, but then I realized this is exactly the kind of '80s social issue that's simply no longer a thing. Kids These Days are all already popular—on the inside. That's because many of us damaged kids of the '70s, who were so ignored we were left to wander our neighborhoods alone for days, have created a reactive style of "do it however you want, Dylan, Mommy loves your very essence" parenting. In this specific school of child-rearing, there's so much parental attention and approval, codependence is solved while the child is still in its third trimester (when they're at their MOST codependent) and their intrinsic value is affirmed daily until they start preschool as blazing ego comets lighting up the sky. Let me be clear, I'm saying this is a good thing. It's definitely way better than the free-range approach our '70s parents took.

And besides having supreme, sometimes unfounded confidence, everything Kids These Days need to know can be accessed online in a five-step YouTube video or some think piece on Vice.com. Younger generations already know not to mix oxy and Seroquel. Many of them own small businesses. God, honestly, fuck off, teens!

I'm writing this chapter for the unsupervised kid. The one who never gets doted on. The one who gets left to her own devices and gets so good at creating coping mechanisms that she never learns to address or fix anything properly. And then suddenly, she realizes she's a grown adult who can't deal with anything. So she gets stuck in a cycle of trying, failing, and then turning to whatever helps her escape the shame of failure. If that goes on too long, the trying part stops and the cycle cuts straight to failing and escaping. When there's no more comfort in the escaping, she'll have to escape from the escapism. And that's when she quits everything and gets super into yoga.

Fine, I'm writing this chapter for me and whoever else wants to not do what I just described.

How to Drink Yourself Out of Having Fun

If you love drinking because it feels like slowly slipping into a big, fun hot tub full of your funnest friends, you're right. It definitely *feels* that way. To you. You're floating along in the therapeutic waters of four beers before the big camp dance. Then "I Melt with You" comes on, and everyone goes crazy with teenaged feelings. You're at the company Christmas party, sneaking shots in your cubicle with that web designer you assumed hated you. Now you realize he's deeply in love with you. "I Melt with You" comes on. Your cubicle goes crazy with teenaged feelings. Warmth, weightlessness, relaxation. What is there not to love?

It's just the thing about partying is that loss of control is one of the major fun factors, but the older you get, the less charming that loss of control reads to the rest of the room. You don't really see it, since you're all glassy-eyed and half-deaf from seven mai tais.

People will try to tell you: "Hey, you humiliated yourself at the Bake-Off and puked in my new Elantra."

And you'll be all: "Shut up, Barry. You're such a drag."

Because it's very, very painful to admit that your party hot tub has turned freezing cold and people are getting out because you've begun to shit in the water. Painful and shameful. Better to attack good friends who care about you than admit you're swimming in a toilet of your own making.

I remember telling a friend I couldn't hang out with her anymore while she drank because it was just like being alone. Or did someone say that to me? Either way, ugh. That was the exact opposite of my drinking goals. I was just trying to get brave enough to invite others in. Sharing the experience once they got there should've been my priority, but at that point, I'd be so drunk I was off whispering secrets to a potted plant, which is uncomfortable for others. Other people's happiness should affect and inform yours. Not in a codependent third-trimester way, but you should care if you're ruining everyone else's good time. Especially if you do that by shitting in your ten-person party Jacuzzi.

This is why they say you can't make a person quit drinking. It has to be their idea. Because really, everyone who stops drinking knows they should've quit five years earlier, but just couldn't let go of the idea that there was perfect fun around the next corner. (Fingers crossed they wouldn't black out waiting for it to come and then punch it in the throat when it arrived, thinking it was a prowler.) YOU CAN'T HAVE FUN IN A BLACKOUT. It's technically impossible, as the definition of fun is probably something like "enjoying an experience." If there's no you there, there's no enjoyment being had.

Here's a helpful drinking to-don't list:

- ✓ Don't get so drunk you make people carry your deadweight everywhere.
- ✓ Don't get so drunk you talk super loud in chain restaurants and ruin a normal family's dad's birthday party.

✓ Don't abandon yourself to the elements. Stick around so you know what's actually happening. It takes discipline, but it's better for you. And if it's gotten to the point where you no longer have a choice, consider getting help. But . . .

✓ Don't keep considering getting help while your life goes to shit, like your friend here.

✓ Don't consider it right into the county hospital, like ol' KK did.

That done, here's your follow-up drinking to-do list:

✓ Take a risk in the *other* direction for once and get healthy.

How to Take Enough Speed to Have the Devil in You

One morning in 1996, when I'd been on speed for about six months, I got up and went for a walk after not sleeping most of the night. I was supposed to be at rehearsal for a sitcom I'd been cast in, but I didn't want to go because I was paranoid thanks to the speed and was pretty sure I was going to die soon. I could tell the speed was affecting my heart rate and I only slept a couple of hours a night. Sometimes the only thing I ate was beer. It had all gotten very extreme. So instead of going to my hard-won, highly lucrative dream job, I chose to go for an early-morning walk around Los Feliz. At one point, I walked by a kind of scary-looking homeless woman and said good morning, and she spat back, "Don't good morning me. You got the devil in you, and I can see it." And I LOST IT because she was right. I did have the devil in me. That devil came in the form of medical-grade prescription diet pills, and they were controlling my mind and killing my heart.

I went straight home and got back into bed, and when my agent called to ask why I wasn't at rehearsal, I didn't pick up the phone, and when I got fired for blowing off rehearsal, I also didn't pick up the phone. And the great irony was I STARTED TAKING SPEED SO I COULD LOSE ENOUGH WEIGHT TO GET CAST ON TELEVISION. And so here was my life, working out exactly the way I wanted it to, and I blew it.

Because I couldn't handle taking pharmaceutical-grade speed daily. Didn't have the grit or the gumption. Didn't have any kind of plan or mentor. Just figured it would work out fine.

No one briefed me on the intense paranoia I would feel about things like friends and phones and white vans parked on my street for more than three hours. No one warned me about the endless tide of rage waves that would sweep over me all day and night, making me almost impossible to be around. No one said, "Hey, this weird plan could give you permanent seizures!" I just kind of went for it.

Now, of course it's humiliating to take a drug and let it ruin your professional life. But the other by-product of being a drunk and/or a drug addict* is that you become terribly arrested in your emotional development. You spend all this time staggering around, singing Alison Moyet songs, and making yourself cry, meanwhile you're not having relationships that teach you how to get better at having relationships. You have "relationships" that last maybe half a night and usually end in a blurry haze and leave a permanent bad feeling in the gut.

---

*   attic

How to Have Regrets

If there's any one regret I have, aside from the permanent brain damage I gave myself that brought with it a years-long anxiety disorder, it's the fact that I didn't learn how to connect with other people well enough to understand that the intimacy you experience in real relationships is a better high than being drunk. I was only having bad experiences with others, as sloppy drunks always do, so I was creating these long shame shadows that I had to constantly run from. I was a human bog. Anyone interested enough to stop and chat immediately felt the ground liquefying underneath them and ran. Maybe I was grabbing at their pant legs too much. Hard to say. I was drunk.

What I do know is that when I finally stopped drinking at twenty-seven, I'd only had two long-term boyfriends—no idea how I snagged them—and in my sobriety, I was mortified by myself at all times.

The hardest part about the first few months of sobriety is that your recent "party" memories come flooding back, most of which are comprised of cringe-inducing fuckups, that then replay in your mind on a horrifying gif-loop. I was horrified the first time I had to sit and listen to the white-wine drunk at the table next to ours talk loudly, be shushed, and then sloppily attack her tablemates. Yes, sister! You have a right to humiliate yourself and others! Fight them all! Fight! Fight! Fight!

I spent a solid twelve years in the bottle. And twelve *young* years. Years that I could've spent learning to play tennis or write fiction or flirt. But no. I chose to seal myself inside the glass medical jar of my fifteen-year-old emotional mind-set. I drowned myself in wine-cooler formaldehyde and put myself up on the highest shelf and kicked over the ladder. And it was a specialty ladder. You couldn't just buy one of them at the mall. Oh, and then I put a sticker on the front of the jar that said, "Don't ever look at this." Then I smoked a Capri and did my best impression of the girl in the "Father Figure" video, even though I have never looked anything like her. The hair was similar, but not the same. Also, she was a model.

What I'm trying to say is that you can absolutely choose to live in a drunken, drugged-out fantasy world. Many do. It's just that, when you're finally forced to come up for air, seeing as it's not a world but in fact a suffocating delusion, you'll find that nothing seems to go your way. (Models are not included in the preceding generalization. Or really ever in what I'm saying. If you're a model, go with god. Enjoy your endless flow of worship and have a great time for the rest of us. Reenact the "Father Figure" video. That's what I'd do.)

People fear sobriety because without the booze, you're forced to see—*A Clockwork Orange*–style—that you're bad at relationships and bad at vulnerability and bad at honesty and your rants about life's injustices are generally not cute. And if you see all that, you have to give up the dream that some brave soul is going to show up and extend themselves to you even though your arms are crossed and your back is turned. You have to stop pretending and start actually earning your keep. It's basic human math. You gotta bring something to the table. You can't just show up empty-handed and expect to be fed.

How to Get Out of Your Jar

The jar sucks. If you've put yourself into one, it's time to meditate on ways to get out. Admit you don't really like it. Admit you're faking it. Consider that there's actually more safety in NOT faking it. That makes me think of my favorite AA axiom: self-esteem is built by esteemable acts.

Why don't they tell us that in junior high? Wanna feel good? Do something nice for someone else. It's all very obvious and yet mysterious and deep at the same time. My fifteen-year-old self doesn't trust it. That's why I try not to let her run things anymore.

I didn't even know she was in charge until I went to—*sing it with me!*—therapy. When you feel totally lost and don't know what to do, it's time to go to therapy. Shop around, find a nice therapist who makes you feel heard, and tell them all your bullshit. ALL OF IT. And then let them tell you what they think you should do. And then try to do it. It's actually kind of simple. That's why it's hard for a lot of people. We're convinced we have to suffer, especially if we've been on our worst behavior for half of our lives.

But that's not a fact, that's a coping mechanism you've (I've) created to make yourself (myself) feel better about doing bad things. It's time to stop doing things that feel bad. But that's going to feel worse because it's new. It's a change. And it'll be rocky in the beginning. This is when you'll really try to tell yourself it's hot-tub time. You'll think, *My hot tub was always fun and great and never had human shit floating in it.* If you're in therapy, you'll say it aloud to another adult who will then say, "I'm sorry. Let's go back—you told me you shit in that hot tub on the reg." And then you'll have to say, "Ah yes. You are correct. I did. Even if I went back now, it would smell like bleach and everyone would give me dirty looks. Thank you for your input. I needed that."

Then the hot-tub fantasy dies and is hopefully replaced by a hot-tub reality. I mean, that's the ultimate goal, anyway. But the difference is, you have to build the reality hot tub by yourself, by hand, including the engine. So you won't get to sink into it for a while. And you'll need to consult with your hot-tub building specialist—the therapist—to make sure you're not fucking it up. Then, after several years of hard work and hard crying, you'll have this thing that will actually hold you as you float in its warm waters of self-acceptance and then "I Melt with You" will come on and you'll feel just fine.

Have I ruined hot tubs for you yet? I really want to.

Ten Starter Ideas for Self-Care Beginners

- Buy any shirt you like that's under ten dollars—you deserve it! (Again, only buy well-made jeans, but get any shirt you want.)
- Make a list of things you're proud of. Continually try to add items to the list.
- If you do something you're not proud of, say you're sorry in real time. This one is hard.
- Practice not reacting to things. Life isn't a three-camera sit-com. You don't need to have a take. You can not know. You can also not care.
- Call an older relative. Generally, they love you and love talking with you. Tell them you miss them. Make them tell you stories from their childhood. Get some other narrative into your life besides your internal dialogue.
- If you're going to a yoga class for the first time, remember you're allowed to be new and not great yet. Try to get the good vibes and fight the need to criticize and compare yourself. Godspeed if you go in for hot yoga. It seriously just seems too hot.
- Work at a food bank, a homeless shelter, an after-school reading program. Extend yourself to others in need. This feels good immediately and gives you perspective.
- Adopt a cat or dog. Come on, you can afford it, you tightwad. Animals make good company while you're learning to become good company yourself.

- Learn to play an instrument. It's something to do when you're alone, and it feels good. If you're not musical, learn to draw. Start to write a book of essays (IT'S REALLY EASY). Put something you've made into the world. It's a good way to practice vulnerability.
- In fact, read Brené Brown's *Daring Greatly*. You'll learn about vulnerability and maybe you'll find your Georgia.

The Top Three Swears and How To Use Them

1. **Shit**: A classic, utilitarian swear that lies on the mild end of the cursing spectrum. Best when muttered under one's breath as a form of self-soothing; worst when yelled at the top of the lungs inside a Starbucks. That means someone who can't self-regulate is sharing a confined space with you, and that is scary. This swear is most fun when spoken by the character Senator Clay Davis in the television series *The Wire*. Go look up a compilation of him saying it on that show and learn swear-based self-expression from the master.

2. **Fuck**: A straight-up red zone swear. This is the word you use when you want to be heard and/or upset your dad at Thanksgiving. Although the force of impact varies from family to family, if you're throwing F-bombs, you're kicking communications into high gear. Very effective with and on children. There's something innately sinister about the sound of the F-word. Whereas *shit* is a quick, light hit, *fuck* is a low gut punch. I think it's that *U* sound in the beginning. It's guttural and threatening, bringing to mind the deep muffler rumblings of a Hell's Angels rally. Dukes up, the F-word's in town!

3. **Cunt**: Well, well, well. Look who we have here. The word that dare not speak its name. The Voldemort of swears. It's the C-word. This swear pushes the cursing needle all the way over into crisis mode. It's a fork-dropper. It's a fight-ender and a silent treatment–starter. Saying the C-word in anger constitutes a verbal scorching of the earth. There's no coming back. And yet, in the UK, I hear they're required to say it three times a day to three different people as they're having each of their three daily teas. (I'm kidding. Don't write in; I know what tea means, ya daft cunt.)

Georgia's Top Ten "Holy Shit!" Moments in Therapy

"Georgia, you worship at the altar of doubt."

My current therapist, Kim,* a lovely, lithe ex-ballerina in her midforties who wears the most beautiful, understated jewelry, said this to me, and when I heard it I could practically feel a new neural pathway forming in my gray, squishy brain. These moments are the ones therapy junkies like me live for. They don't happen often, but when they do, they remind you how much there is still to learn about yourself. Bombshells like this one, if processed correctly, can lead to becoming a happier, healthier person.

I've been going to therapy since I was six, which means thirty-some-odd years of new neural pathway revelations. Therapy has been a part of my life since I can remember, a lot like acne and that one black wiry hair on my chin. It's actually a red flag when I'm *not* going to therapy, as it's a sure sign I'm avoiding something in my psyche. As someone who's introspective to a fault, I find it delightful in an absurd way every time I have a new revelation. Even after literally

---

* Sadly, Kim passed away in 2018, during the writing of this book. See dedication on page 5.

decades of being in therapy, I still have major realizations about why I behave the way I do or why my emotions do what they do. Having those "OMFG, I GET IT!" moments in therapy are really thrilling to me.

OK, because my OCD (legit diagnosed!) brain loves lists and organization, here's a list of ten things I've gleaned from my lifetime of therapy.

10. It's important to have someone to emote to, even if it's someone you're paying.

I remember in vivid detail the day my dad moved out of our house for good. He only took a few things with him—clothes and a couple of framed photos. Most of the furniture pieces were hand-me-downs from my mother's side of the family, and all the decorative touches were made by my mom during the few years she got to fulfill her dream of being a housewife. That dream was over, but you could hardly tell anything had even changed, let alone that a family was being dismantled.

My heart broke a little bit a couple of times that day. It first cracked when he walked out the door. I begged him to stay. Then again later when I grabbed his pillow from off what had been my parents' bed and clutched it to my chest as I lay on his workout bench. He'd later come back for the bench once he had a place to live. When my mom caught me crying while taking deep inhales of pillow, which still smelled like my dad's musky, piney aftershave, she told me to put it back. "It isn't your father's anymore."

Later that evening when he finally called to let me, Asher, and Leah know he was OK, all I could hear was the huge world he was now inhabiting by himself echoing through the line. I didn't have the ability to imagine him anywhere but home with us, but he was out in the chasm of dark night, where danger lurked in every shadow. He was supposed to be home with us, watching TV with a can of Bud Light sweating in his hand until dinner was ready, then we'd all sit around the table eating and talk about our day. Then maybe we'd play a board game or watch TV as a family. If it was Friday night, Shabbat, we'd light the candles and he'd lead us in a melodic prayer, a blessing for "a good week, a week of peace" the words in a language I didn't understand but whose power I still felt in my bones.

But over the past year those family evenings had happened less and less while the beer cans had become more and more, and instead of board games and prayers, our evenings were filled with a tension, the language of which I also couldn't understand but felt even deeper in my bones.

When I said good night and hung up the phone the house felt empty and unfamiliar. My heart broke for the final time that day, and truthfully, I don't think it's ever fully recovered. Divorce, man, it's a fucking bitch.

After he moved out and the messy divorce proceedings began, I took to hiding in the cozy closet under the stairs (remember how I Harry Pottered with Ray Bradbury under the stairs? Yeah, Harry Potter definitely didn't exist at that point, so I'm not a copycat.).

The dim light from the bare bulb overhead was soothing and cast deep shadows off the shelves of dusty board games and extra bedsheets. It felt like a world all my own, where custody battles and sibling rivalry didn't exist, and *James and the Giant Peach* wasn't a fantasy but could maybe be my reality.

I'd make a comfy bed on the floor with the blankets my grandma Thelma had knitted, each in coordinating tacky '70s colors—brown, marigold, maroon, you know what I'm talking about—and happily plant myself with James, the giant peach, and my trusty cat, Whiskers, for some solid "leave me the fuck alone" time.

I had found Whiskers abandoned as a kitten the year before, and she had quickly become my best friend and confidante. Looking back, my mom letting me keep her was probably a "fuck you" to my severely allergic dad, but I was still too young to understand spite. Whiskers lived to be twenty years old and is my touchstone for what a perfect cat is: purry, snuggly, sometimes aloof, sometimes needy, prim and proper, funny, and silly.

I guess the constant crying and locking myself in the closet for hours on end was a red flag even my mother, devastated and preoccupied with her own newly chaotic life as a working single mother of three shell-shocked kids, couldn't ignore. So she made an appointment for me to see a child psychologist.

From what I'd seen in comic strips and TV shows I was too young to be watching, going to a psychologist meant getting to talk about yourself while you lay on a comfy leather couch and then someone would tell you why you did the things you did or maybe analyze your dreams. You know, like going to a psychic but for your present-day self instead of your future self. I was *so* excited. Going to a therapist felt like such a grown-up thing, and as the youngest child in any family knows, getting an hour of uninterrupted time to talk about yourself is an unimaginable luxury.

In walked Erma, a soft-spoken, poised woman who was pretty in an unassuming, kindergarten teacher way. She had a calming effect on me, with her flowing clothes draped off her in an unfussy yet classy fashion. She had an almost undetectable South American accent, and her soothing voice and dark, intelligent eyes made me want to speak to her in confidence the way I only had with Whiskers.

Looking at photos of myself back then, it's hard not to feel sad. Rail thin with huge eyes circled with unnatural dark rings from the anxiety-induced insomnia that I've never been able to shake. The ill-fitting hand-me-downs that my skinny body practically swam in, stringy hair that I hated to comb (still do), an unconscious posture that screamed, "Don't look at me!"

The therapy room was different from what I had imagined. Instead of a wall covered in framed degrees from fancy universities, there were children's drawings and posters of kittens in baskets, which I found babyish and immature. Rather than heavy tomes, there were colorful kids' books and puzzles and simple games. I had been hoping for something more mature, something more scholarly, something that screamed, "Mental health!"

But I'm pretty sure we didn't draw, or read, or do a puzzle that day. I'm pretty sure I just sat on the small, child-sized couch and cried. It was never an explicit rule, but crying in my house wasn't an option for me. I cried when I was frustrated with my mom who I now know was yelling because she was frustrated with me. But crying felt like I'd lost the battle. Crying in front of my older siblings didn't draw out any sympathy either. It was just another reason to pick on each other.

So just crying, just showing my sadness to this person who

responded with soothing, positive affirmations and comforting palliatives was a huge relief.

9. Not all therapists are alike.

In later sessions, Erma and I did do those puzzles and draw. After a few more sessions, which of course I didn't understand at the time were a way to get me to open up and talk to her, I asked her why we couldn't have a normal, "grown-up" therapy session. I think I even asked her if we could have a "real" session. "You know, like on TV. Where I lie on a couch and you ask me questions and study my mind and interpret my dreams."

Guys, I was precocious as fuck. She obliged, and we had one session in the office next door to the children's room, the room reserved for grown-up sessions, complete with framed degrees and giant books and not a single kitten poster.

No bullshit, I'd trade five years off my life to listen to that audio or travel back in time and observe that session with little me.

Erma was my first and best therapist. Like Whiskers being my point of reference for a good cat, Erma is my point of reference when deciding if a new therapist is a good fit for me. In the thirty years since I first met her, I've sat down in those grown-up offices with dozens of therapists and can usually tell in a matter of minutes—maybe seconds—if I'll be coming back for a second session. Everyone's looking for something different in a therapist. For me, it's a knowing look in their eye that speaks to a good mix of compassion, strength, and warmth. I've had good therapists who I didn't click with who I only saw for a couple of sessions and not-so-good ones where we sat in silence for fifty minutes. Fifty minutes is a long time of silence, especially when you're paying for it.

The point is, it's important to find a therapist that you can find a rhythm with, and not to get discouraged when it takes a few tries. Just as you're not going to become best friends with every person you meet, you're not going to click with every therapist you meet. But when you find one you do click with, just like when you find someone else who loves murder and will talk with you about it for hours over tuna melts and black coffee, it feels fucking fantastic.

8. A diagnosis ≠ disaster.

I've been diagnosed with many different things throughout the years, but I've come to the conclusion, with the help of my current therapist and psychiatrist, that my mental ailments are a delicious mix of the following:

Georgia's Brain Cocktail
    1 oz. generalized anxiety disorder
    ½ oz. depression
    2 tbsp. ADHD
    a pinch of OCD

- Pour into a shaker filled with ice and shake until well blended. Pour into a beautiful vintage glass and garnish with abandonment issues and 25 maraschino cherries.

I know a lot of people who freaked out when they got diagnosed with anxiety or were told they're bipolar or whatever. Here's the thing, firstly, most insurance companies require a diagnosis before they approve treatment, so keep in mind that your therapist might just be generalizing or rounding up to the nearest common demoralizer. Second, I'm a big believer in finding out what the hell is wrong with you so you can start working toward relief. Just as you want to locate cancer in the early stages, the sooner you find out what's going on with that brain of yours, the sooner you'll be able to find the proper treatment so you don't let your issues reach critical mass.

ADHD, hypochondria, depression . . . these are all diagnoses that, if not treated, can lead to you running your fucking life amok and just being a general bummer to be around for both your friends and yourself. But! They're also all diagnoses that respond incredibly well to treatment. So you have a choice. Either find out what the hell your major malfunction is and then go about trying to make your life better and worth living, or don't do that and keep your head in the sand and then complain all the time to anyone who will listen about how annoying it is to have tiny rocks in your fucking teeth all the time.

7. A diagnosis ≠ a comfy jacket.

The truth about depression is that it, for me, can sometimes be comforting. It's like an old familiar jacket that you know you should get rid of cause it smells like mothballs and Cheez-Its but it just fits so well and you've had it all your life so it's sort of nostalgic and soothing, even though it stinks. Sometimes when I'm super overwhelmed by life and need an excuse to shirk all my responsibilities, I find my inner monologue telling me how depressed I am. So even if I'm not currently depressed, if I'm just stressed or tired or in the mood to eat cookies and watch TV all day, I'll metaphorically throw on that stinky coat and wallow in its itchy, familiar fabric.

Is this making sense? Basically, instead of labeling myself as someone who *suffers from* depression or anxiety or whatever, I have to remind myself that I'm actually trying to *thrive with* depression or anxiety or whatever. I can't use my diagnosis as an excuse to throw a protective barrier over myself or an invisibility cloak to hide from life. It's time to throw that coat, and this coat metaphor, away and use more productive tools to cope. Ya know?

6. You don't need motivation.

To be fair, this was said to me by a life coach, but same diff. I had never considered calling a life coach before because my overly cynical self winces at anything hippie dippie and New Agey. To me, a life coach was just for people who didn't have the balls to go to *real* therapy and face their *real* problems.

But then I was talking to a successful lady friend of mine about how depressed I was about never getting anything done. Now listen (look), I'm a hustler and I work hard, but being a lazy person is my default. It's what I do best. I'm a champion napper—I've even taken a nap in the Louvre among other weird places. I love chilling and day drinking and taking it fucking easy. But as it turns out, I'm not retired just yet, so I try my best to go against the lazy grain, which is why I always have multiple to-do lists going. Otherwise, I'll to-don't with everything and take a nap instead.

So my friend, who by all accounts has no problem with getting her ass into gear and taking care of business, told me her secret weapon: the life coach she'd been working with for the past year. Being the self-care junkie that I am, I had this life coach's number in my phone within seconds and called her later that afternoon to set up an appointment.

At our first of what would be many sessions, I was bemoaning the fact that I just couldn't seem to get anything done and I was using the tired excuse of not having any motivation—to go to the gym, to write, to get out of my pajamas some days.

"I just keep waiting and hoping that the motivation to do all the things that I genuinely want to do, that I *should* do, will hit me so I can stop being depressed about being so lazy," I told her.

Her response was a slap in the face of obviousness that was so true it had never even crossed my mind: "Motivation isn't necessary," she said. "You just have to *do it.*"

Yes! That makes so much sense. I can drag my ass to a spin class and hate every moment of it, but I still *did it.* I'm writing this chapter even though I just downloaded the audiobook of Michelle McNamara's *I'll Be Gone in the Dark* and all I want to do is listen to it while I paint my nails, but deadlines are a thing, so I'm writing down the top ten biggest therapy epiphanies of my life like a boss instead. I'm not motivated, but these words! They just keep showing up on my screen!

Point being, you don't have to bound into every situation ready to kick ass, you just have to show up, and once you're there, you might as well do your best. But fuck it all if you think I'm not taking a nap afterward.

5. Be kind to little you.

There's this Instagram-famous girl that I've met a few times who's gorgeous and kind and has really pretty hair who would post a #tbt pic of herself every Thursday throwing back to when she was a chubby little girl with some kind of cruel caption making fun of herself for how fat she was. And it broke my heart. The little girl in the photo looked so innocent, and there was something about the look in her eye that reminded me of my own low self-esteem as a child, and the thought of that little girl, who probably got made fun of a lot, finding out that her gorgeous, grown-up self with really pretty hair would also be making fun of her someday just didn't seem right.

And I do it to myself, too, but in a different way. At some point in my childhood, I learned to be very mean to myself. I regularly call myself a "stupid fucking idiot" in my head when I'd do something as simple as take a wrong turn, forget my sunglasses, or can't think of a third example in the book I'm writing. But then my therapist helped me understand that the impatience and exasperation I felt toward myself was a learned behavior that I picked up from a childhood of being treated with impatience and exasperation by outside forces, but I didn't need to continue that cycle.

She told me to picture little Georgia, at five years old or so (when this behavior was learned), and imagine calling her a "stupid fucking idiot" for making a mistake. It made me want to cry. Five-year-old Georgia doesn't deserve that; she deserves understanding and patience and to know that mistakes can be made without them making her a broken person. And so when I berated myself for that wrong turn, I was perpetuating the narrative that Georgia doesn't deserve to be treated with kindness. Even though I didn't start it, the only person who could stop that cycle was myself, and a great way to do that was to picture myself as a little kid when I was being cruel to myself. It's taken some time, but I've definitely been kinder to myself since I learned that.

And I commented on internet-famous girl's Instagram account that it made me so sad that she was mean to her little self, and you know what? She stopped posting mean comments with her #tbt pics. I'm really glad. Little her, and big her, didn't deserve it.

4. Beware of the altars at which you worship.

My current therapist Kim,* who specializes in cognitive behavioral therapy (CBT), is sweet, soft-spoken, and generally very chill. Our sessions are discussions more than hard-core psychoanalysis, which means she doesn't often give me her opinion unless I specifically ask for it; she just leads the conversation to a point where I understand

---

* See page 173 and dedication on page 5.

what's truly going on. So it was really surprising recently when, after doing her signature staring off while mulling over my response, she looked at me and said, "Georgia"—which is always jarring when your therapist directly says your name—"you worship at the altar of doubt."

I felt like I'd been hit by an emotion truck. That one little phrase encapsulated so much of what I had been showing up with for the year and a half that I'd been seeing her. I subconsciously make sure I never believe in anything, like a forced nihilism, because doubt feels so much safer and reliable than faith and optimism.

Stupid people are optimistic. Positivity is for cheerleaders and youth group leaders. I'm negative and cynical, man. It's part of who I am. It's punk rock and gen X, and it's someone who can't be fucked with. But it turns out it's a defense mechanism so I'm never disappointed, just pleasantly surprised when good things happen.

We all have our core beliefs that protect us from that which we're too scared to admit we want, like love or money or happiness, as if we'll somehow jinx our lives by thinking it. It's fine to not want to scream it to the sky, but make sure you aren't cursing your own happiness by believing more in something never manifesting, by worshipping at the altar of doubt, or negativity or obliviousness, than actually trying to attain that thing.

3. Look for the proof.

"I'm lazy and incompetent."

"Everyone hates me."

"Everything is hopeless."

These are all easy things to say to yourself when you're depressed, but when you let a therapist know you're feeling this way and she asks for the proof otherwise, it's usually pretty easy to spout out a list of all the ways these negative thoughts aren't true.

"I worked my butt off today and watched one episode of something on Discovery ID. That doesn't make me lazy."

"I have an active social life and close friends who care about me."

"I have no idea what the future holds, but so far the future has been pretty good."

When you stop and hold yourself accountable for those negative thoughts by challenging them, they hold less weight. The more often you prove them wrong, the less control they'll have over your mood.

Having anxiety makes it so there's a running tally in your head, kinda like a stock-market ticker tape, of all the things you've done wrong, will do wrong, how things can and probably will go wrong, and just general ways everything is fucked. It becomes really hard to live a life that has any semblance of normalcy when that tape keeps fucking tickering at all hours of the day.

I know very few people who don't have some level of anxiety, however miniscule, and my husband, Vince, is one of them. He falls asleep when his head hits the pillow at night, instead of lying there for three hours worrying about not falling asleep like I do, and he wakes up every morning and starts fucking singing instead of worrying about everything he has to do that day! Singing!! Thank god opposites attract or he would have been terrified of me. He thinks logically—he looks for

proof—and so far in his life, logic has proven to him that everything is going to be OK, even when everything is currently very fucking shitty.

2. You have to balance the negative with the positive.

I'm allowed to be negative and cynical and worried that I'm going to get hit by a car or that a stranger on the street is going to throw acid in my face, but it's only fair that if I'm going to give those thoughts time (give the doubt and worry a voice) that I then have to give the opposite (the positive) the same amount of time.

For example: "My career is going to implode in my face and everyone will hate me." Yeah, OK, but you're resilient and strong, and your husband and family and cats will never hate you. "An airplane is going to crash into my apartment building, and the flames will slowly engulf me and my cats." Airplanes rarely fall out of the sky, and the likelihood that it'll happen to you is statistically zero. Plus you'd die on impact, so the fire part wouldn't matter. "Vince is going to realize what a nut I am and leave me for a normal girl who doesn't worry that he's going to leave her for someone else and also remembers to eat breakfast every day." Vince knows you're a nut and actually likes that part of you! Plus he's a little nuts in his own special way, and you think it's charming and cute, so that's probably what he thinks about you, too.

OK now you try it.

1. It's OK.

Recently I had plans to meet up with my mom. We were going to have a fun lunch at a cute café where we'd drink a few glasses of crisp white wine, get table fries, and I'd tell her all the awesome stuff going on in my life and ask good questions about hers. But instead of her being at the designated place at the designated time, she ended up getting very lost. And I got increasingly pissed off when her phone kept cutting out as I was trying to tell her which way to go and she refuses to use GPS cause she doesn't trust technology, and she couldn't figure out how to turn on speakerphone because she wouldn't pull over and get her bearings cause she's impatient. I was there at the cute café, but instead of bonding with my mother and housing some table fries, I was screaming into my phone, "PULL OVER, PULL OVER!" and ended up yelling, "JUST GO HOME!" and hanging up on her. I got back in my car and turned the radio up really loud and scream-cried to whatever was playing on the radio. Green Day, I think, which is very good music to scream-cry to, it turns out.

When I saw my therapist after the scream-cry lunch incident, we broke down my anger and impatience at my mother's behavior that day. What it boiled down to for me was simply lateness. Specifically, my extreme, soul-crushing fear and hatred of lateness.

I was late a lot as a kid—to school, to temple, to my own grandmother's fucking funeral.

It was always "FIVE MINUTES UNTIL DEPARTURE" as my mother ran around the house like a lunatic (and you know how we feel about being a lunatic . . .).

Then, on our way to wherever we were late to, she'd bring that lunatic business into the car, speeding to make up the time we'd lost. She'd apply her makeup while driving, so she only kept one unmascaraed eye on the road while other drivers would honk angrily at us and cut us off in a rage. It was terrifying.

When we would finally show up—twenty minutes late minimum, which my mom simply referred to as "Jewish standard time"—whatever we were arriving for would've inevitably already started. The image I have filed away under "lateness" in my mind is everyone turning around from something—their desks in my classroom, the synagogue pews at temple, the funeral service of my beloved grandmother—to stare as we quietly, embarrassingly shuffled in and mouthed our apologies to the people who knew how to get places on time.

Twenty years later, I was running late to therapy with a tough-as-nails woman I only saw for a couple of sessions. Running late, as you've probably guessed, is one of my biggest anxiety triggers. I'm pretty much never late, but it doesn't matter; I'm stressing out the whole way over and probably making some pretty dumb and dangerous maneuvers while driving to avoid being late. The honest truth is normally when this happens, I end up ten minutes early to meetings, sweating, and then have to wait twenty minutes for the person I'm meeting because I'm the only on-time person in LA.

So when I arrived five minutes late to therapy, sweating, and over-apologizing, my therapist said, "Georgia, I don't care if you're late. You could be forty-five minutes late. You're paying for the hour, so you can do whatever you want with it."

I told her about how cruel I was to myself when I was late or even just thought I might be late, calling myself my standard "stupid fucking idiot" and generally admonishing myself in a way I would punch someone in the face if they said the same to me.

She looked at me wisely and said, "What do you think is the mentally healthy thing to say to yourself instead?"

I guessed wildly, because the answer seemed so obvious and I should just fucking understand: "Calm down! Dude, chill the fuck out!"

With each guess, she shook her head.

Finally, I gave up, and she said in a soothing, calm voice, "It's OK."

I started laughing at its simplicity and how it had evaded me. So now I use it all the time. When running late, "it's OK." When I have a million things to do and not enough time to do it, "it's OK." When I get stuck in a fantasy about plane crashes or normal girls, "it's OK." It's my mantra when I need to override the voice that tells me that nothing I do is OK.

Introspection brings up messy crap, which I think is why it's so hard for some people to get themselves to go to therapy at first. Sometimes we're just not prepared to even *think* about the messy psychological bullshit, let alone unpack it and start to sort through it.

It's like when you get a facial because you have acne, but the facial itself brings up all the gross crap under the surface of your skin, which causes you to break out more as it eradicates itself, but eventually the end result is glowy skin with fewer blackheads.

Side note: therapy and facials are two of my favorite self-care things. Coincidence?? Probably.

Don't Be a Fucking Lunatic: Final Thoughts

KAREN: What's your favorite form of escape?

GEORGIA: Reading and yoga are the only two things that really get me out of my head. I tend to think too much and worry a lot, but reading takes me into a totally different world where there's no room for my own bullshit. I know I've found a good book when I realize I've been completely transported to a fictitious place while reading.

As for yoga, if I don't concentrate, I'll fall on my ass, so that's good motivation not to be distracted by how badly I need a pedicure or if I locked my car.

KAREN: Anything you were a huge fan of when you were younger that you now can't believe you ever liked?

GEORGIA: So much stuff, including going to raves, loud music, drugs, roller-skating, staying out all night, smoking cigarettes, Long Island iced teas, emotionally unavailable dudes, boot-cut jeans, tube tops, body glitter, lying out without SPF.

KAREN: What's the weirdest situation you ever got into because of drugs or booze?

GEORGIA: For sure the time my then boyfriend and I ate pot and went to an amusement park. I got too high and broke my brain. I'm pretty sure the park employees knew we were high and were fucking with us, because the ride we were on broke down in the middle of an intense section involving monsters, and they left us there with the horrible singsongy theme music playing on repeat in our locked seats for like ten-plus minutes. I freaked out.

After, we went to "chill" at the Muppets 3-D movie, and I couldn't move my body and was convinced I had been brainwashed by the CIA via the Muppets. When I finally got myself moving and ran toward the theater doors, hitting all the poor people in the row in front of me in the head with my purse, Miss Piggy yelled from the screen, "Get her! She's getting away!"

Oh, also I chewed up a crayon while on LSD because my friend and I thought it would make our spit look really pretty. It did.

art by Claire Mabbett

6

GET A JOB

KAREN: "Get a job" was the first step in the three-part process I once blurted out while we were ranting about the importance of personal safety. Self-sufficiency is your first form of self-defense. The sooner you accept that you must work for a living, the sooner you can roll your sleeves up, find your true calling, stack that paper, and spend the rest of your days singing along knowingly to every Destiny's Child song.

Karen's Dos and Don'ts Guide to
Becoming Employee of the Month

If you work in Hollywood long enough, and you don't go insane and drive your Range Rover off a parking structure, you'll inevitably be asked the following question by someone who wants to work in your profession: "Can we get coffee sometime so I can pick your brain?" They will actually say the words *pick your brain* as if it isn't the grossest and most invasive image of all time. Sure, come dig around in my mind. The key that unlocks the golden door of show business is definitely in there somewhere.

It was much worse when I worked on a popular TV show. You wouldn't believe the asks that came rolling into my in-box—people I barely knew explaining that their son or daughter had recently graduated from college and was now interested in taking a job in television. It was all I could do not to reply, "And are you going to do the job for them? Because as far as I can tell, you want it more than they do. Sent from my iPhone."

Now, it wasn't that I didn't *want* to help people. I was just saving all my help for people who actually deserved it. And I was surrounded by those people every day. There was a roomful of interns who'd gotten there by signing up for a college internship program. They were chosen out of hundreds of applicants. Those bright young minds moved from all over the country to Los Angeles to spend months cleaning the office kitchen and loading paper trays and carrying pallets of bottled water up and down stairs FOR FREE. For fucking free. The ones who didn't quit or get cut eventually moved up to production assistant (PA) positions. And if they were good PAs and stuck with it, there was a chance that they might get promoted into the department they wanted to work in. That entire process took at least two years. Those were the people who deserved a leg up. They'd earned it.

Wait, were you ever a PA or an intern, Karen? No. Shut up. How dare you. I paid my Hollywood dues in a different way. It was not as noble as the journey of the humble intern, but it was on par. You see, when I was twenty, instead of applying for an internship program at my college, I flunked out. My loving parents had no choice but to cut me off, so for about six months, I lived in a white-hot, flat-broke panic. And then it came to me: I had to do something big to prove I wasn't the flunky loser that reality was making me out to be. So I decided to become a stand-up comic.

This really seemed like a solution to me at the time. I'd always wanted to do comedy, and I'd studied every stand-up comedian's act that I'd seen on TV since I was ten. I figured I'd start, work my way up in the clubs, and then become rich and famous. It was a three-part plan. Easy peasy.

But it turns out, that plan didn't have three parts. It had like, two hundred and fifty. It literally took me fourteen years to "make it" in any real, bill-paying way in show business. And in the meantime, my job choice was constantly being questioned by my parents, my friends, their parents, my parents' friends, just about anyone who wandered by our house and heard what I did for a living. I was told it was impossible. I was told to be realistic. I was told I needed a safety net and that nobody made it in show business without connections. None of these people who were talking had ever worked in show business. Many of them had never been to LA for more than a weekend. But they sure knew how it all worked. And how it wasn't going to work out for me.

This is when I learned a valuable lesson: anyone trying to give you career advice is full of shit, especially if it's a family member. People hear about you trying to do something they were never brave enough or lucky enough to try. You making a go of trying to make your dreams come true makes them feel bad. Maybe because they had the same dream. Maybe because they had a mean dad who made them become a stock analyst. Now they see those small decisions dictated the shape of their lives, and it makes them feel disappointed somehow. Whatever the details are, they're projecting all their old shit on you. Step away from these people gingerly. Do not engage.

Because it doesn't matter if you fail. Your trying is what sets the tone for your whole life story. Think of everything you do as being chapters in your future autobiographical self-help book about murder. Your "career" is just another word to help you categorize the journey you will take through life. Why not start brave and bold and believing in yourself? And if you fail in the thing you want to do, that's fine. You can start your career-having life in one career, and then if you need to, you can switch to another. I did.

After I'd lived in LA for six years, I was at the end of my rope. I was still doing stand-up and getting auditions here and there, even a small part or two, but the initial magic I experienced was clearly drying up. I was totally broke and didn't have any prospects. I called my dad for yet another loan. This time, he didn't yell or lecture me. Instead, he very sadly said, "Honey, I think it might be time for you to throw in the towel." I waited to be heartbroken, but it didn't happen. In that moment, I knew he was wrong. I didn't hope he was wrong, I was positive. I told him to give me a couple of more months. It was spring. At some point, my friend Jay Johnston got a producing job on a new sketch show for the WB. He told me to put a packet together and submit it. I said I didn't know how. He said, "Yes, you do." I got my first writing job at the end of that summer.

I separated this sidebar so it didn't screw up the flow, but I should note here that there were many people in my life who always, always believed in me. My grandma Grace, who used to make me stand up and sing at the dinner table when I was three; my aunt Kathleen, who used to make me stand up and sing at family parties when I was twelve; my uncle Rich, who always told me how talented he thought I was; my sister, Laura, and her best friend, Adrienne, who never said anything to my face but showed up for practically every single comedy show I ever did; and my mom, who used to chuck me under the chin and say, "Whatever it is, you've got it, kid." I will also include my father in this group, because, although he was in a constant state of worry over my lack of job skills and all-around instability, he always let me know that he admired my bravery and he celebrated every one of my showbiz victories by declaring loudly, "You did it! And you did it without knowing anybody!" Of course, this isn't true. The only way you get anywhere in Hollywood is by making friends with people who like you enough to get you jobs. He meant that I wasn't the spoiled child of some movie star or studio head.

OK, now back to changing careers midstream even though you've invested years in one particular arena.

Frequently Asked Questions Right Up Top:

Q: Is it hard to change jobs?
A: Yes. But so is everything.

Q: Will it take a long time?
A: Of course, dummy. Nothing worth it doesn't.

Q: If I switch careers, won't it mean that I'm a failure and everyone on Facebook will laugh at me?

A: Yes. No. So what. Get off Facebook. That shit's for the birds.

Now that there are definitely no more questions, here are some vague lessons I learned from the *other* glamorous jobs I've had:

Horse Stall Muck Person

To the twelve-year-olds who didn't listen earlier when I told them not to read this book and are still waiting for dead body pics, this one's for you: don't let adults guilt you into being their indentured servants.

When I was around nine, the lady down the street hired me to muck her horse stalls after school every day. I think she paid me ten bucks a week and I never got snacks, but that wasn't the worst of it. These horses were kept in a tiny stall strung up with an electrified wire top rail.

That right there should've been sign enough that I, a small child, was not qualified to deal with these particular horses. The lady had explained that she didn't want them rubbing against the stall entry, but—and I only just thought of this now—who buys a horse and leaves it in a small pen all day only to have a child come and walk it for an hour after school? That's horrible. I feel like any qualified horse person would not approve of her setup. If any animals should be free range, it's horses.

But I wanted my own horse so badly, I was willing to do whatever it took. I figured if I could prove that I could take care of one, my parents would buy me one for Christmas or my birthday or just because they loved me. They had explicitly and repeatedly told me they would never, ever do that. But maybe they would. My mom would always wink at me and say, "You and your expensive tastes."

She was right. I really have always had an eye for the finer things. If there were five sweaters on a table, I'd pick the imported cashmere. I've always loved bleu cheese since I was like six. I once told my parents if anything happened to them, I wanted to live with my aunt Michelle because she had such a nice house. Also, while I have you here, I'm realizing what a big winker my mom was. If you have kids, I really recommend winking at them conspiratorially. It's fun and special, and the overall effect lasts for years. Ugh, I miss my mom.

OK, so as you could imagine, by the time I got to these horse stalls every day, the two horses were DYING to get out of their stalls. Just going nuts in a very intimidating, *Legend of Sleepy Hollow* sort of way. The high-pitched whinnying and stomping of their front hooves was downright biblical and legitimately dangerous. These horses were so scary *I never learned their names*. And I was a nine-year-old girl! I must have known they were only going to break my heart.

They weren't like my aunt Jean's horse Lady, the horse I grew up riding, who was so nice you could currycomb her for an hour and she'd never move. Lady was the best. She looked like a horse from a sexy horse calendar, chestnut brown with the white star on her forehead and pretty, long bangs.

She was infinitely patient, except when you saddled her; she always did that horse trick of bloating out her stomach so it wouldn't be too tight. One time she did that, and then my cousin Stevie put me on the horse with him and ran Lady around the field at a full gallop. It was super fun until the saddle started to slide over to the left more and more. Right before we fell off, we were riding perfectly horizontal to the ground as she trotted along. She was good enough to stop walking when we fell off. She had a real "You crazy kids!" attitude, and she loved alfalfa. God bless you, Lady. You were good people.

OK, so back to these other scary horses.

So here's what I got to do in my childhood horse-taming-cum-stall-mucking job. First, I took down the impossibly taut electric wire, then I put their bridles on and walked them out of the stall, then I mucked the stall while the nameless horses grazed on the grass around the barn, and then I put them back. I shocked myself with that fucking wire every day. And the horses knew I was nervous, so they'd usually bolt when I opened the door. I got very good at walking them out the doorway, then dropping the rope and jumping aside so I didn't get dragged along or trampled when they took off. IMAGINE A CHILD HAVING THIS JOB TODAY. Or even an adult. Like, fuck this lady.

So then, one day I show up and the wire has somehow come down and one of the horses has gotten its leg tangled in it. It wasn't electrified, thank god, but the horse was losing its shit and had been for a while. I ran and got my aunt Jean, who cut the wire and then let the horse out. Then she started asking me questions about my "after-school job." That night, she told my mom this lady had given me WAY too much responsibility. When the lady came home and my aunt told her what happened, she tried to *blame me* for not putting the wire fencing back properly in the first place.

My aunt lost it, because her trying to pin that on me meant the lady hadn't checked on the horses herself in a full day. I mean, I'm sure she was also offended that a grown woman would accuse a child of mishandling electric fencing, but that was a subtler aspect of her argument.

Anyway, I just remember when the yelling started, I knew I wouldn't have to do that job anymore. I remember dropping to my knees in the rain and thinking, *HALLELUJAH PRAISE JESUS,* but that might just be that scene in *The Shawshank Redemption* and not an actual memory. I remember my mom being really upset and telling me to please tell her the next time I was ever in over my head like that. I said I would. (Cut to a montage of me having many assorted "wild horse" problems and not telling anyone over and over for the rest of my life.) After that, my interests turned to watching TV and staying very still for hours at a time. Like Lady with her currycombs.

Shoppe Clerk

Here's the thing: if you have an obsession and it's for a thing, don't get a job at the place where they sell that thing. Like, if you're a blackout drunk, don't work at a bar. Don't hang out at the barbershop if you're trying to grow your bangs out. Don't get a job at a tuna cannery if you're a cat. I wish someone had said any of these things to fifteen-year-old me before I got a job at a frozen yogurt shoppe.

When frozen yogurt made its big splash in the mid-'80s, I couldn't believe how great it was. I wanted to eat it all day. And as a nation, we all believed it was the healthy alternative to ice cream. We believed it was nonfattening. We were fools. The cool girls at my high school started getting jobs at the new frozen yogurt shoppe in town, How Sweet It Is. It was fun and easy, but when I worked there by myself, I could not stop eating the strawberry yogurt. It was tart and cold and hit me somewhere deep inside. I only wanted that taste in my mouth for the rest of my life.

Now, my eating disorder was in full swing at this point, so I had begun to deal with all the heartache and social stress of high school by eating. And eating. And eating. I wish I'd known at the time that this was pretty much standard fare for teenage girls. But I didn't, so I burned with shame, angry that I didn't get the food issue that makes you skinny and light-headed and just as ashamed. I got the one that convinces you the best way to deal with things is to be alone and binge-ing. Ideally on fast food. I despised myself for being so hungry all the time and despised my face and body for showing the effects of my indulgences. But the other girls who worked at the yogurt shoppe either didn't have my problem or dealt with it in a different way. And I still had years to go until I was to discover sex and drugs.

For a while, food was the only high I could access, so I abused it terribly. I hadn't realized how much until one day when I had the afternoon shift and our boss and the owner, Thelma (not Georgia's grandma), stopped by the store. She was having meetings with people and doing some yogurt shoppe business. I'd cleaned all the things I was supposed to clean and no one had come in, so I served myself a small strawberry yogurt, posted up on a stool, and read a book. There's no way Thelma liked that, but she didn't say anything. Nor did she say anything when I helped myself to more yogurt. It was only when I went for a *third* refill did she ask me in a frustrated tone to go wash the dishes. I was baffled. I mean, didn't she tell us we could eat the yogurt? What was her problem?

Thinking about that now, I am cringing so hard my shoulder blades hurt. I was so dumb and spoiled. IT WAS A JOB. I was being paid. I didn't just overeat her product, I did it in front of her WHILE

READING *THE STAND* BY STEPHEN KING. And I never thought to myself, *If I'm doing here what I do on vacation, there's a chance I'm being a bad employee.* Then one day, my two friends and I had a shift together and we carved our initials into the fudge, even though she expressly told us not to touch it. The frozen yogurt shoppe to-don't list was one item long. I was fired soon after. I was definitely embarrassed, since the other girls were not fired or fat, but also incredibly relieved to get away from the temptation. Also, no one makes frozen yogurt that way anymore, so it's not as good as it used to be. Thank god.

Person Who Works at the Gap

This was definitely one of the worst jobs I've ever had, mostly because, as I made clear in my yogurt shoppe hijinks above, I think I'm above working in any way. I think I'm better than being gainfully employed. And based on my love of bleu cheese and horses, there's a good chance I was a royal in my past life. But even if I were a common peasant, working at the Gap sucked. They paid minimum wage, only scheduled you part-time, and they expected you to say hello to every single person who walked in the door. Ugh, how gauche. Working there barely covered my rent, so I never had any money left over to buy any of the clothes I stared at and was required to dress in all day.

Retail sucks. It's genuinely hard work and it pays like shit and no one appreciates you. Meanwhile, the CEO of the Gap at the time—I keep wanting to say Donald Fisher, but that could be wrong—was in the news once a week for how much he'd increased sales and revenue for the company. I've been living proof that trickle-down economics are bullshit since 1992.

It didn't help that we had to listen to the same thirty songs for eight hours straight. That was maddening. I mean, so much Enya and Enya-like behavior on that playlist. And there were so many rules and regulations. So much prodding to be a better salesperson, to add on some socks, to intrude and "help" people. I hated all of it. I only wanted to work at the Gap because my friend Dave already worked there, and I'd just moved to San Francisco, so I wanted to inherit all his friends. I wanted to do the easiest thing I could (see: yogurt shoppe story) in the most painless way possible and leave fifteen minutes early.

But the Gap was for go-getters. It was for people who fought over who got to be the greeter, who never felt awkward barging into a fitting room to really assess the fit of some weirdo's hideous jeans. The Gap was for assistant manager hopefuls. I just wanted to phone it in.

So standing on the floor of this clothing store filled me not just with boredom but with a certainty that I was going to work there forever. And that certainty filled me with a dark fear. It scared me so badly I became compelled to try to get stand-up sets around town. You need to have an engine to get anywhere. The fear of stagnation can be a very powerful one. So I started to really try. I called in and signed up and did everything I could to be like a "real" comedian. The ones who didn't have shitty day jobs. The ones who sat around writing in coffee shops in The Sunset for hours and hours and had new bits every night. *Someday*, I would whisper to myself, standing at the dressing rooms, staring at piles of ugly striped rugby shirts that I had to fold.

Someday.

Georgia on Working for the Weekend and Also Free Snacks

I got my first job the moment I was old enough to get a work permit from my high school guidance counselor, the minute I turned fifteen. Yes, having an after-school job meant I could skip sixth period and get out of class early, but I was a regular ditcher, anyway, so that wasn't what was important to me. What I wanted, what I had dreamed about having since I was a kid, was pure and simple. Money.

I knew that money meant freedom and the ability to make my own decisions. No longer would my mom be able to tell me that I couldn't buy the king-sized Reese's peanut butter cups at the grocery store or that knock-off Doc Martens were just as "hip" as the brand-named boots, which we all know is total bullshit. I could buy whatever I wanted, and eating cheese fries from Del Taco and buying cigarettes from the one gas station in town that sold to minors was my dream life at that age.

My preferred brand was Marlboro Reds, but the cheapest were an off brand called Smokes, which was written in a really cool old-timey font across the package. I think they cost ninety-five cents or something crazy like that. I'm sure they were made of pure asbestos and paint chips.

I wish I'd known how good it was back then, not needing to pay rent or have a car to get around (I lived in a very walkable town). If I'd known that I was going to have to have a shitty, entry-level job for the next fifteen-plus years until I stumbled into internet success, maybe I would have waited a couple of years before entering the workforce. Probably not, though. Those cheese fries weren't gonna pay for themselves.

But really, I've always liked having a "job" job. It made me feel like a productive member of society, like I was an adult. Despite having dropped out of school for court reporting, cosmetology, psychology, and early childhood education, I never really pictured an actual "career" as something I was worthy of. Careers were for smart people who had the patience to sit through class and the self-discipline to do homework. I thought I was dumb, and my patience is not and never has been go—OH HEY, LOOK AT THE PRETTY HUMMINGBIRDS!

Where was I? Oh, right. Here are some jobs I've had.

Shop Girl

Unlike Karen, I loved working retail. I have a bit of a shopping addiction to begin with (see: my closetful of vintage dresses), so being around clothes all the time and being up on the latest trends was pretty awesome for me. Granted, I couldn't actually *afford* any of the trends, as I was always paid somewhere near minimum wage, but every once in a while, I'd have a cool manager who would slip me a blouse I'd been eyeing as a reward for a particularly good sales week.

At eighteen, I worked at a clothing store on Melrose Avenue that sold generic factory-made ladies' clothes that they had bought in the garment district downtown and sold at a 300 percent markup.

When I was twenty, I was hired as an assistant manager (a fancy way of saying I got paid a dollar over minimum wage and had a key to the stockroom) at Hot Topic. It was in the dark corner of a mall that was empty most of the day, so I'd kinda just wander around the store and pick out things I'd buy if I had more money. It was actually pretty fun, since my coworkers were all cool burnouts like I was. But then one day, my new boyfriend, who I was out of my mind in love with, dropped by to see me, and I left with him to go get a part for his new Vespa in Compton, and I never went back. The boyfriend ended up SUCKING (more on him later), so I'd actually have been better off staying at Hot Topic, which is something no one has ever said in the history of Hot Topic.

After he dumped me, as my heart was still in the process of piecing itself back together again, I got a job at a vintage shop in Santa Monica. It was a large, kinda fancy shop that had great clothes and sometimes celebrity clientele. The owners were a husband and wife that had come into some money and clearly had never owned a clothing store before. They were never not bickering about the business. It was a total mess. The shop employed a few other girls that ended up becoming some of my best friends for a few months and were instrumental in helping heal my broken heart.

That job ended when six of us decided to become roommates and moved in together in a converted janky office building in a bad part of town and swiftly couldn't stand each other. We all went our separate ways after that.

Lunch Lady

I am truly a whore for food, and I freaking love it. Food is my favorite hobby. I've waited tables and did the unavoidable Starbucks stint, stuffed my face with cookies behind a bakery counter, and washed dishes in a fancy restaurant.

The weirdest food job I ever had was as a lunch lady at a school for troubled kids when I was twenty-three. It was basically an offshoot of the Los Angeles school district for kids grades three through high school who for behavioral reasons couldn't hack it in regular public school. I'd gone to a similar school in my hometown during a particularly hard and rebellious year of high school, so I felt right at home. It was a small school, one classroom per grade, and I quickly became a fixture and got to know the kids by name, and they me. I'll never not love being called "Miss Georgia."

Every morning, I'd pick up the kids' breakfast and lunch for the day at the regular school, then hand out each meal classroom by classroom at the appropriate time.

One thing you should know about me is that, while I fucking LOVE eating at fancy restaurants and know a ton about gourmet cuisine, junk food is my PASSION (I'm literally eating gooey mac and cheese at my favorite café while I type this). Maybe it's because my parents were health nuts, so growing up, it wasn't just stuff like sugary cereal and soda that were off-limits but also processed food like white bread and mass-market peanut butter. I didn't have a proper classic white bread, mustard, bologna, and shitty American cheese sandwich until I was out of high school. My mind was blown.

Unfortunately, the school food was all processed-to-hell chicken nuggets and pepperoni pizza with gobs of greasy, plastic cheese product. The food in the shitty rehab I was at when I was thirteen was better than that trash.

At the time, I was a broke community college kid and had just moved in with a boyfriend for the first time. Before I met him, I'd never weighed more than 105 pounds in my life due to a variety of eating disorders, which meant that at five foot five, I was a scrawny mess whose head was too large for her tiny frame. I'm not saying that that weight is inherently unhealthy (everyone is different!), but as an adult who doesn't starve herself, I know that if *I'm* doing things right, my comfortable weight is somewhere around 130–135. That weight means I'm happy, healthy, and taking care of myself (and also that my tits aren't nonexistent). At 105, I was none of those things.

But somehow, after I passed out all the prepackaged Uncrustables for breakfast or bean-and-cheese burritos for lunch, there would inevitably be a leftover serving. I didn't want it to go to waste, and I was broke, people! So I'd eat whatever was extra, and even though it was trash food, I fucking LOVED IT. And slowly but surely, I gained weight and filled out, until one day when I met my dad for lunch, upon seeing me, he exclaimed awkwardly and happily, "Oh! You're filling out!" I laughed my ass off but knew what he meant. I looked like how I was supposed to look. And I liked it. I had cleavage and hips and even that little under-chin pooch that I hate but try to ignore.

Office Drone

My last job before I was lucky enough to quit and give entertainment the old college try (which thankfully requires little to no college) was as an unhappy, slacks-clad office drone when I was in my late twenties. I was a receptionist at a multibillion-dollar corporation staffed by the same boring WASPs I had so happily escaped post–high school. I hid my large tattoo on my calf under pants I bought at a thrift store in high school for four dollars that I'd hemmed with duct tape and whose zipper was held in place with a safety pin because I REFUSED to spend any of the little money they paid me on business-casual work clothes. I was depressed as fuck and thought that this was my future. I truly thought that for the rest of my life, I'd be a low- to mid-level employee at some nameless company, never making enough to save for retirement and eating breakroom granola bars for lunch till I died. I'd get drunk with equally miserable friends every night because I was so unhappy with my day. I'd take hangover naps under my desk during my lunch break or wander around downtown LA and break a sweat to release myself from the layer of air-conditioning that kept me shivering at my desk on the thirty-third floor of the high-rise that I was SURE was going to come down in an earthquake. I was fucking miserable.

I started blogging to relieve my boredom. I've always loved writing, and blogging was an easy way to "get pen to paper," even though neither are involved. I'd write about stupid stuff and funny stuff, sentimental bullshit, and random stuff I was interested in: cooking and clothes and cats, and all the gritty shit I had gone through in my life. Nothing was off-limits, I was a born blogger (read: an over-sharer). It was a lot like the essays you've been reading in this book, only now I know the difference between *your* and *you're* and have a really great editor so I seem super litterit! Thanks, Ali! [Editor's note: Your welcome!]

Blogging got me out of my rut and made me feel like I had a purpose but was also a great way to put a positive spin on my life. When my car got broken into one morning and my stereo stolen, my first thought wasn't about how much it would cost to fix it, it was, *I can't wait to blog about this!* I joined the first and only dating site I used knowing that even if I didn't meet the love of my life (spoiler: I didn't), at least it'd be great blog fodder. And instead of sleeping during my lunch breaks, I'd go outside and take cool pics of my cheap, homemade lunch and the book I was currently reading, and then post them on my blog. I learned to play the drums, dressed up in my favorite vintage dresses on the weekends so I could post the photos, and taught myself to decorate cupcakes like a pro.

When my best friend and I made up a gross, inside-joke cocktail that we called the McNuggetini in the summer of 2009, I insisted that we actually make it so I could blog about it. That turned into a funny how-to video that we shot in my grandma Thelma's kitchen (she was the one who made all my Harry Pottering afghans) with the help of a friend who had a video camera, and we were shocked to see the view count explode when we posted it on YouTube. When we got a message on Facebook from a dude at Cooking Channel who asked if we wanted to make more tongue-in-cheek cocktail videos online, I quit my job to give myself a chance at doing something *real*. Something for me. My only goal was to never go back to the thirty-third floor. It's been nine-plus years, and so far, I've been able to make ends meet doing things I love: a food and travel show on Cooking Channel, recurring narrator spots on *Drunk History,* and later, a podcast about murder with my tuna melt friend, Karen, that's made my life blossom (like a goddamn field of wildflowers shot in that shaky fast-motion style) into the insanely wonderful career and community it is today. And look at me! Now I'm writing a fucking BUK! [Editor's note: Your doing great!]

My grandma Mollie's favorite saying was "Bigger dummies than you." That admittedly somewhat-cynical saying has been my motto pretty much my entire adult life. It applies to so many different aspects in life. Bigger dummies than I am have written a book. Bigger dummies than I am have made a fulfilling career despite not having graduated college. Bigger dummies than I am have beaten their eating disorders. So why the hell not me, too?? I don't claim to be better or more talented than anyone, but I do know I deserve just as much of a chance at a happy life as everyone else, and I think I deserve that chance because I'm not a shitty person, which really is the point of life in my eyes: "Don't be a dick and do good things." That's my other motto. It has the word *dick* in it.

Can we have a sincere moment of vulnerability for a sec? You guys, oh my fucking god, I am so lucky that my life turned out the way it did. The word *gratitude* doesn't even begin to cover it, and I can't imagine there will be a time in my life when I'm not in awe of what has happened—namely, this podcast. It changed my entire existence. While your job doesn't define you as a person, who you decide to bring to the table (or desk, cash register, classroom, whatever) does have an effect on how you interact with the world. So if you're doing a job you totally hate and that makes you feel small, you're going to bring that feeling with you everywhere you go. That makes for a pretty miserable world.

I don't know, if I have to give some sort of advice here to all you sweet baby angels who want more than how you're currently living, I'll say, just remember that as long as you're attempting to not be a dick and doing your best to do good things, you're worthy of a good life, one that you're proud of and that when you wake up every morning makes you stoked to be yourself. And if you don't wake up stoked to be you, figure out the first step you can take toward that life you want. Once you've taken that first step, then figure out the next step, and so on. It might feel like a long journey (it is), but for me, that was the most important part, because once I got to where I wanted to be, I was confident in my ability to grab that opportunity by the balls and make it my bitch.

Get a Job: Final Thoughts

KAREN: What was the first career you ever seriously considered and why?

GEORGIA: I really wanted to do hair and makeup when I first got out of high school. It seemed like a chill, creative field where I could be myself and actually be excited about the job instead of just being a working stiff for the rest of my life. I ended up dropping out of beauty school three months in, but it was a super fun three months and I'm still pretty good at cutting my own bangs!

KAREN: What's the hardest job you've ever had?

GEORGIA: The hardest jobs are always the ones you don't really like. So while this podcast and everything surrounding it (oh, I don't know, say for example: writing a FUCKING BOOK) is insanely hard, I feel so lucky that I get to do it, so it doesn't *seem* that hard. But really, though, it's made my hair gray and made me double up on therapy and the stress has probably taken a few years off my life, but it's made the years I do have so much better, so I'm at peace with it.

KAREN: If you had to get a new job but you weren't allowed to do anything you've already done before, what line of work would you go into?

GEORGIA: I think I know myself well enough at this point in my life that I'm just not cut out for school, so it would have to be something I'm already qualified for like bartending or crime scene cleanup. I've always thought raising and training cadaver dogs would be fun.

Or! Maybe I'd open a sandwich and pastry shop that also sells vintage kitchenware and has an outdoor bar where people can bring their dogs and babies and there's also Skee-Ball and Scrabble. Man, that sounds like a perfect place. I bet your cult would hang out there.

BUY YOUR OWN SHIT

art by Abigail Ervin

7

BUY YOUR OWN SHIT

GEORGIA: This goes along with the theme: There are no shortcuts in life. That the easy way is, in fact, never that. When you don't act with the understanding that no one can take care of you better than you, you can find yourself in a lot of trouble, living a life that you don't control, or trusting people with nefarious intentions. Just like the saying goes, "There's no such thing as a free lunch," meaning if it seems too good to be true, GTFO of there.

Georgia Demonstrates the Zen in the Art of Being a Crazy Ex-Girlfriend

The acute pain you feel when you get your heart broken . . . have you ever felt it? Oh my god, it fucking hurts. There is no escape from it, no amount of pills to help you fall asleep and sleep well, no amount of busyness you can fill your day with that'll block out the raw, constant pain, and it's *physical* pain, I swear.

I, of course, learned this firsthand many times, so by the time I was eighteen, I thought I was an old hand at heartbreak. By that point, I had been through multiple relationships, having started dating at the tender age of thirteen. By the time it was my turn to dump someone—my first real boyfriend when I was seventeen—I was very gentle about it, knowing from repeated experience how it feels. The guy I dumped right was Chris, who I mentioned back in "Send 'Em Back." We'd met in rehab and had basked for a year and a half (an eternity for a teen!) in all the boyfriend/girlfriend goodness that I had always fantasized about, like referring to each other as "babe," having sleepovers when my mom was out of town (complete with my first orgasms!), and spending Christmas at his house with his big, totally normal family, who treated me like family, complete with my very own stocking hung over the fireplace. It was the first time in my life that I understood why people actually wanted to get married and have kids. I could see having that with him, but when it came down to it, I wanted something totally different in life.

So I decided to create my own breakup model, in which I'd act in the way that I wished the guys who broke my heart had. The whole idea can be summed up by the camping mantra, "Leave it in the condition that you found it." To sum it up even more bluntly, "Don't be a dick when you break up with someone." Essentially, straightforward, honest, and clean is the only way to break up with someone and have you both leave with your dignity intact. No ghosting, no months of breakup sex, no hemming and hawing and toying with them. This takes a TON of vulnerability because this process is awkward as fuck and feels shitty to both parties involved, but I swear if you buck the fuck up and break up like a civilized person, in the long run, unless they're a psychopath or total dick, you'll keep your soul somewhat unscathed and their ego and heart not broken beyond repair.

But then at nineteen years old, I met Aiden, who I fell for hard and fast as only someone who thinks they're immune to heartbreak does. *Blindsided* is how I would best describe it. It was the late '90s, and I'd finally (*finally*) moved to Los Angeles from my hometown of Orange County. I thought my life was beginning and that adventure and freedom would be around every corner. And then I turned a corner one day and I found Aiden. Hot, well-dressed, tattooed Aiden.

Less than a week after getting handed my high school diploma by Principal Who'd-Have-Thunk-It, I passed through the Orange Curtain and moved to my gloriously gritty, smoggy, unpredictable Los Angeles. You remember this part. This is the part where after eighteen long years of the stifling blandness and uniformity that is suburbia, I'd finally come home.

Being in a city where I knew no one was terrifying and exhilarating. I would drive around aimlessly in my first car, a bare-bones, hand-me-down Toyota Corolla whose after-market budget speaker system was somehow connected to the stick shift so when you shifted up, the radio got louder, and when you downshifted, it got quieter. So just picture eighteen-year-old Georgia in hip-hugger jeans with dyed black hair and a lip piercing screaming along to gut-wrenching emo songs about longing and heartbreak, daydreaming of all the life-changing events that my future had in store.

Every new neighborhood I'd find in my wanderings made me feel like an explorer uncovering uncharted territory that I'd mentally mark on my map, always expanding upon the geography of my adopted hometown.

Beverly turns into Silver Lake. Rowena turns into Hyperion. Hollywood turns into Sunset.

This was when online directions and maps were in their infancy and definitely not available on my archaic pager—yes, I had a pager; no, I wasn't a drug dealer—so my back seat was littered with discarded printouts from MapQuest, which were usually incorrect and definitely a driving hazard as you'd have to read the tiny printed directions and navigate LA's traffic at the same time.

Driving in LA is and always has been a feat of bravery, something best left to sadists and those of us with a Xanax prescription. Bumper-to-bumper traffic is the norm, at any time of day, and one out of every three drivers is a raging lunatic asshole who doesn't think the rules apply to him because he has lots of coke and a car that could pay off your student loans. The stress and idiocy and left-hand turns with no arrows is enough to make a Buddhist monk lose his chill. No joke, sometimes when I'm alone in the car, I roll up all the windows and scream at the top of my lungs just to release some pressure. I've spent entire therapy sessions talking about how to control my anger while driving. It's A LOT.

Road rage aside, the first step to my fabulous new life was getting a job on Melrose Avenue, at the time my favorite place in the world. Back in the '90s, the famous Melrose Avenue was a gritty, graffitied, eclectic street that, for about eight long blocks, was home to cheap-as-fuck thrift stores, gay sex shops, record stores, and cafés serving terrible coffee.

Adding to its weirdness was a retirement home smack-dab in the middle of the action, whose occupants would post up in their chairs on the sidewalk every morning for a front-row seat to watch the mix of shoppers and homeless people and delinquents with mohawks as they paraded up and down the avenue.

Just a few blocks west was the high school where my parents met as teens, but this was *my* Melrose that housed the tattoo shop where I got my underage, Ray Bradbury–tribute nipple piercing and my pink '70s prom dress for twenty-five dollars (a splurge for me then). Throughout high school, I maintained an expertly balanced rebel esthetic of '60s grandma dresses paired with spiked dog collars and used Chuck Taylors by making twice-yearly pilgrimages to Melrose with my sister in her beat-up 1988 Toyota, on which she'd painted a giant psychedelic butterfly across the side. I officially bestow my heartfelt thanks to the gods of fashion who must have been watching over us, due to the fact that we never stalled on the 405 during that hour-long journey. I mean, that car was a fire hazard. At best.

But Melrose . . . (takes a deep breath, extends arms, and spins in a circle) . . . this was our weirdo home base. I collected every Dead Kennedys album from the various record shops dotting the block. It was a hub for those of us who didn't fit in and had no desire to do so.

So when I moved to LA and started looking for a job, the store didn't matter as long as I worked on Melrose. That should explain how I ended up with the official-sounding title of assistant manager at the first shop where I had turned in a job application. I was paid in cash under the table every week (in a mini manila envelope, to boot) but they let me blast Modest Mouse over the speaker system, so I looked the other way.

During my lunch breaks, I'd visit the shops along the block despite the fact that I was paid a pittance, so I couldn't afford to buy lunch, let alone a vintage purse that I coveted from a shop down the block that was adorned with a giant peacock made from colorful rhinestones.

So one afternoon during that first summer in Los Angeles, 1998, I ducked out on my lunch break, and it was a perfect, perfectly LA day— sunny and warm, but not scorching yet. One of those lovely days that convince you that everything is right in the world. I'd brought my lunch that day, so I had a couple of bucks in my pocket, which I promptly used to buy a used Buddy Holly cassette for my car and its defective stereo before making my way down to window-shop at one of my favorite vintage spots, Jet Rag.

Every month, Jet Rag hired someone to style their four or five window displays, and whoever it was that they used was wildly creative and talented. Using only items in the store, they would create these tongue-in-cheek scenes that were more like dioramas that belonged in a macabre museum than measly store-window displays. But on this particular day, the thing that caught my eye wasn't the fancy window art, it was the scooter parked out front.

It was a beautiful old Vespa, and even though I didn't really know what Vespas were exactly, I knew I loved them. I had of course seen Audrey Hepburn looking adorable jetting around on one in *Roman Holiday*, and I knew I loved the way this one looked parked on the sidewalk, ready for adventure. I coveted it. I had never been a person to have any interest in riding a motorcycle (anxiety doesn't love it when you take risks), but this cute, kitschy scooter was begging me to don a vintage dress and take a Sunday ride along the beach. It spoke to freedom from the claustrophobia of my car.

As soon as I walked into Jet Rag and saw Aiden, I knew he had to be the owner of said Vespa I coveted. And I coveted him, too. They were a perfect set—the beat-up vintage scooter of my dreams and the cute, quiet older guy with the Rude Boy aesthetic complete with worn-in Doc Martens and suspenders holding up his fitted jeans. His head was shaved, tattoos covered his slender, sinewy arms, and his coke-bottle eyeglasses made me want to protect him from schoolyard bullies. He had adorably crooked teeth and a slight limp from what I later found out was an old scooter accident (see, my anxiety was right!) and I was smitten-as-fuck at first sight.

I grabbed a random dress off a rack and walked over to the dressing room counter he was manning.

"Hi, can I try this on?" I asked in my most charming voice. As he walked me back to an empty dressing room, I casually asked, "So is that your Vespa out front?" He said it was, and I told him how much I adored it, which seemed to stroke his ego, and we shared a flirtatious smile as I closed myself in the dressing room.

Once I was securely behind the curtain, I wrote my pager number down on the back of the receipt for the Buddy Holly cassette I'd just purchased, and when I brought the dress back out to him, I handed him my number as well. "Call me," I said, and then I sashayed my capri-pant-wearing ass out of the store.

Jesus, I was confident back then.

I only had to daydream and fantasize about being on the back of Aiden's Vespa for one day before he contacted me, although my aching want to have that Vespa, OK fine, and also *him,* between my legs made it feel like an eternity. So basically, I did the crush thing I eventually became mature enough to know not to do: I let my fantasy of him become more important to me than who he turned out to be for real, which was not that great and also kinda boring.

The first time Aiden and I hung out, I met him outside of Jet Rag when his shift ended, and he handed me his extra helmet. It was a vintage WWII-style black helmet that I later learned is nicknamed a "brain bucket" by those in the know due to its ability to do absolutely nothing of use in a crash aside from keep one's brains contained instead of spilling across the asphalt. As an adult, I'm having a panic attack just writing that.

"How does this work?" I laughed as I struggled to figure out the clasp beneath my chin.

"I got it," Aiden said with suave confidence as he tucked his (much safer) helmet between his legs and moved heart-racingly close to me to help secure the helmet.

I held my breath and took his moment of distraction on the clasp to study his face. Lovely dark lashes surrounded his sky-blue eyes, and his lips were the pillowiest I've ever seen. Just as I felt gravity pulling me toward them, the clasp was locked in place and the moment had passed.

"There!" he said in triumph, and he put his own helmet on, straddled his scooter, and motioned for me to hop on back.

"Remember this moment, remember this moment," I mantra-ed to myself, knowing this, my first-ever motorcycle ride, would be something I'd want to remember in the future. And I'll be honest, I wasn't totally sure it wouldn't be one of my last memories, as the anxious girl in me wasn't completely convinced we weren't going to crash and die that night. I hoped we'd at least get a chance to make out before that happened.

We took off from the curb with a jolt and were flying down Melrose Avenue, passing all the familiar shops and personal landmarks, but this time, instead of being safe in my bubble of a car or slowly walking along the sidewalk, I was free and open and it felt like I could reach out and touch something. The road, a store, the sky, whatever. I felt like I had been wearing a heavy coat my whole life, and suddenly, I was wonderfully, refreshingly naked. Add to that the exhilarating feeling of having my arms wrapped around the waist of this very attractive dude, who I'd been fantasizing about and flirting with over the phone for days. It was overwhelming. I was dizzy.

I pressed my nose to the back of Aiden's leather jacket as we zipped in between cars idling in the late-evening rush-hour traffic, and I inhaled the intoxicating aroma of vintage leather, made all the more exciting by the fact that my last boyfriend, an Orange County bro with the least

Rude Boy aesthetic on the planet (what's up, dreadlocks and nipple piercings), had been (deep, cleansing breath . . . wait for it . . .) a vegan.

I had never experienced that shocking freedom that comes with being exposed to the world on a motorbike or the envious looks from the normal people, in their normal cars, living their normal lives. All these things conspired to make my heart race that much more when we later kissed on an empty beach in Malibu, his Vespa abandoned by the road, waiting for us like a spaceship in the moonlight. We rode for hours, late into the freezing-cold night with the single headlight illuminating the road in front of us. Down Sunset Boulevard past the designer stores and huge billboards, through the winding roads that are lined with some of the most expensive houses in the country, and all the way until it deposited us on the Pacific Coast Highway. By the time he dropped me off in front of my grandma's house, I was so cold I could feel it in my marrow. I felt like I'd never be warm again, so I ran a steaming hot bath and soaked until the shivering finally stopped and my fingertips were shriveled. I went to bed that night, on the same mattress my mom used to sleep on as a child, with a smile on my face, still feeling the vibrations from the scooter throughout my body.

This is how my fairy-tale Los Angeles life began. This is what I had waited eighteen years for under the stairs in my childhood home, reading while wrapped in an afghan, with Whiskers asleep on my feet. It was happening.

Aiden is from a time in my past I can never get back and never want to. It was the time in my life before I learned that when a guy is quiet, when he seems intellectual and all-seeing with a rich inner life but shy and reserved, it's actually because he's boring. Or worse, he's hiding something. I now know that both of those things were true in Aiden's case, but at the time, his silence intrigued me and gave me the opportunity to project whatever I wanted and needed him to be onto what I thought was this brooding, deep person.

Quick advice break, friends and fiends: don't project your own fantasy and personality on shy people. Let them speak for themselves, or in shy people's cases, not speak for themselves. If you're like me and can't handle one-sided conversations and pulling teeth to get someone to open up to you, go find someone who will.

I imagined Aiden's inner world to be deep and complex, and I wanted to be the girl he opened up to and shared his thoughts with. In reality, it turns out he was just concentrating on how to keep his long-term girlfriend a secret from me the whole time. Womp womp.

Don't mistake someone's quietness, lack of participation in a conversation, or—worse—air of disinterest as intriguing. If someone holds their cards close to their chest, it doesn't necessarily mean their cards are worth fighting to see. The people who are open with their cards, who wear their cards on their sleeves and offer them to you in a take-it-or-leave-it manner, those are the people worth playing cards with. I don't know why this metaphor has become a card game—maybe it's been too long since I've been to Vegas—but you get the gist.

And hey, if you're shy and hold your cards close to your chest, I get it. It's hard to open up to people, especially when you've been hurt before and you were raised in a house where your caretakers were emotionally unreliable or used your emotions against you because of their own untreated psychological issues (Wait, what? Mom??), or because someone in your past didn't adhere to the "leave them like you found them" breakup model.

On my second date with my husband, Vince, I was so irritated that he was being quiet that I told him I couldn't keep hanging out with him unless he started talking. The night we had met, we had talked animatedly all night, so I knew we had a good connection, but as soon as we started dating, he clammed up.

After a date that I cut short 'cause I was just so sick of hearing myself talk and ask him questions to try to get him to talk, he asked me if everything was OK via text.

"Can I call?" I texted back. I wanted to level with him and it didn't seem fair to stop seeing him without giving him a reason and a chance to fix it.

So in the back of the bar where I had been drinking and commiserating with a friend, I called him and decided to be vulnerable.

"I need you to talk," I bluntly told him. "I have a really hard time with silence and quiet people. It makes me talk too much and I hate having one-sided conversations and I know you're probably just nervous, but talking too much makes me hate myself. Also eating in silence gives me a panic attack" (one of the last leftover symptoms of my eating disorder).

Vince laughed and apologized and promised he'd start opening up, blaming his quietness on nervousness because he liked me and didn't want to screw it up.

"I'm one of the goofiest people you've ever met once you get to know me," he told me playfully.

"Prove it," I flirted back. He did, and he is. I even included my love for his goofiness in my wedding vows.

When I look back to my months-long relationship with Aiden, there were so many warning signs and red flags that I willfully ignored. The constant look of tension on his face even while he professed his love for me. The slight hesitation every time we kissed. Just those two things should have been enough . . . but I was young! I was trusting! And back then, I believed in my daydreams and fantasies more than I believed in listening to my gut (see "Georgia's Take on Red Flags and Riot Grrrl Courage"). I don't mean that you should ignore your fantasies, but there's a healthy balance that we should all be striving for in life. Not many eighteen-year-olds have that balance yet, so back then, I fell quick, I fell blindly, and most of all, I fell hard. I fell in a way that I later worried I'd never be able to fall again, but at the same time hoped I wouldn't, so I could spare myself the pain.

The night Aiden dumped me, I knew it was coming. *Ghosting* wasn't a term yet, but that's what he was trying to do to me. You gotta laugh in the face of a dude who thinks he can ghost a desperate, obsessed eighteen-year-old girl.

"HAAA!" I said to myself as I paged him over and over and over. We could only page with numbers, no words (what was this, the fucking Dark Ages??), but we had codes to get a message across. Paging someone with the code 143 meant "I love you," so I blew his pager the fuck up with those three little numbers. I called his work, I called his home, I called his friends. I was embarrassed for a long time after about my behavior when he dumped me, but as an adult, I'm like, "Fuck that guy!" Clearly he didn't leave me as he had found me. I wasn't a broken, blindsided teenager who felt like the biggest fool on the planet when I met him.

When he finally realized he wasn't gonna be able to slip quietly into the night, he called me at home, and as I sat on my mother's childhood bed, on the same now-faded brown-and-teal-striped sheets from Sears that she had slept on, he told me that he had a girlfriend and couldn't see me again. I cried and begged him to see me one more time so I could convince him that he loved me, but he hung up on me.

At that moment, at the tender age of eighteen, I built a wall around my heart. One that would take several relationships and over a decade of therapy to dismantle enough that I could have a relationship in which I didn't use this wall as a point of reference. My relationship with Aiden validated the fears that I'd had since childhood: that I wasn't enough, that I was stupid and everyone knew it, that my capri-pant confidence was a joke. Those validations just made my heartbreak so much worse.

It was the point in my life when I realized that dudes who talk about their "crazy ex-girlfriend" are full of shit. What they're really talking about is someone they hurt and didn't leave the way they found. These guys put their ex-girlfriends in a position that makes them do things so extreme and out of character that they seem crazy. The night Aiden called me, after months of "I love yous" and making plans for our future, and told me he had a girlfriend and couldn't see me anymore, and then hung up? By dawn, I was parked outside his work, I hadn't slept the entire night, and I waited for him to show up because I needed an explanation in person. I didn't get an explanation. I just seemed crazy. And in that moment, I *was* a little crazy. Love is supposed to make you feel a little bonkers and batshit, but there's bad crazy and good crazy, and you realize which is which when you love someone who doesn't love you back.

Cut to a couple of deeply depressing months later, when I bought myself a present that initiated my slow climb out of that hole: a tattoo. Two red hearts, the size of silver dollars, on either side of my upper butt. Like mud flap décor. The tattoos (my first real, professional tattoos) that I got while I was still grieving his bullshit were a welcome distraction. They took my mind off the emotional vacuum that my life had become; they were the first thing I had been excited about in months.

After what seemed like eons of heartache, the pain slowly dissipated. I was able to make sense of it and see myself as the protagonist in the story, not as the stupid, foolish love interest. I stopped looking for him in crowds, stopped dreaming of running into him, stopped imagining some magic bolt of electricity hitting his brain, causing him to realize the error of his ways and beg for me to take him back.

But what I didn't get over was the feeling of riding through my adopted city on a purring scooter with the wind in my face, the smell of two-stroke oil, and the snug fit of a (safe, up to code) helmet on my head.

So after six months of squirreling away those little envelopes of cash I'd get from the shop every week, I'd saved enough for my own vintage Vespa.

She was so beautiful, straight out of an Audrey Hepburn picture. An ET3 Primavera, dark blue with baby-blue trim. This loud, crowded city is empty like the apocalypse has come and gone early Sunday mornings, so although I am and always have been a late sleeper, my excitement for that scooter had me up at the crack of dawn on Sunday mornings for months so I could have the city to myself for a while and just get lost on my scooter. It was my church.

I'd ride for hours and find new neighborhoods and new shortcuts. I'd laugh out loud when I'd pass a bunch of cars at a stoplight or shimmy through stopped traffic. I rode east into unfamiliar neighborhoods in Hollywood, Los Feliz, and Echo Park, all neighborhoods I would eventually live and love in.

I learned the layout of my city on that scooter, and I gained my confidence back by having bought my own shit.

Breakups will make the best of us go fucking batshit, but if you learn through it that you can rely on yourself to mend, you'll go a little less crazy each time they happen. By the time I met Vince, I was a confident person who, while wanting a relationship, didn't stake my personality, my dignity, and my life on it. It became a nice addition to an already lovely life instead of a mad, needy thing that identified me like it had with Aiden.

Almost ten years after I got my scooter, which I'd long since sold when I realized how dangerous and risky riding was, Aiden added me

as a friend on Facebook. I was momentarily stunned. I hadn't heard from him since that awkward, tearful confrontation where I demanded an explanation on zero hours of sleep. By then, I had gone through so many other things— years of happiness, good friends, and a trusting relationship—I had a better grasp of the world and my place in it. We chatted a little online, like normal old friends, and I realized he was just *some guy* . . . that's it. I realized, for the first time since then, that I was over it . . . I even said it aloud to myself, just to make it real (something I do every once in a while). That feeling of freedom made my heart skip a beat, just like it used to when I'd ride on my Vespa.

Karen's Advice on How Not to Be Thirteen Forever

I'm not sure how it started, but I had a bad habit in junior high of asking people to give me things: a bite of their Snickers, thirty-five cents so I could buy my own Snickers, whatever it happened to be that lunch period. It was usually Snickers-related. And I always asked one of the shyer girls in my class. They were usually pretty low-key about it. I certainly couldn't ask my loud best friend, Hannah. She'd just bitch endlessly about how her mom never gave her money and how I was spoiled. And I was spoiled. But I was also very addicted to sugar and the jet engine of my eating disorder was just getting warmed up, so I did what I had to do to get my Snickers-related fix.

Now, I was new to this Catholic grammar school and found it to be a deeply creepy place, inside and out. The first- through eighth-grade classrooms were all housed in the "new" building, a two-story, cement leviathan that was built in the '30s. It was cold and dark and echoey, with high ceilings and lots of paintings of Jesus looking super bummed out at you. The plot of land it sat on took up almost an entire city block and included the original school that had been built in 1888—the year Jack the Ripper terrorized London. Not that I knew about that at the time, but I was definitely getting a Victorian England vibe. Maybe that was because between these two large, ominous buildings lay a rectangle of asphalt lightly covered in gravel and that was our playground, not a blade of grass in sight. Or a swing. Or a monkey bar. Just some faded yellow lines that had been painted onto the asphalt decades before. And to up the weirdness factor, although the buildings themselves were level, the playground was on about a twenty-five-degree angle. So whatever you were doing, you were either walking downhill or uphill. That aspect gave you a strange, boaty feeling that kept you permanently off-center. It was as if they'd plowed the land to specifically make fun a chore, while maximizing our skinned-knee potential. I did not like this school.

All along the east and west perimeters of the playground, there was one continuous low bench where every kid in the school had to sit and eat lunch by grade. Then, when the bell rang, the younger kids jumped up, screaming, and ran around. The older boys played intensely vicious games of dodgeball. But the older girls simply sat on that bench in groups of three and five, whispering and stewing. The school was comparatively small, about forty kids in each class, so the line between popular and unpopular had long since been drawn and was clearly defined. I arrived in sixth grade with all my country-school Montessori confidence, thinking I would fit right in. Reality quickly taught me otherwise.

The girls in my new class were sharp-tongued and distant and shockingly uninterested in my fascinating personality. On my second day there, I overheard one girl say to another, "Ew, look how greasy her hair is!" while making a face right at me. I was floored. After that, I washed my hair every day and stared in the bathroom mirror every night, searching for all the other flaws I hadn't been noticing. But this was junior high. The only rule was the rules kept changing. You were never safe. It was the perfect breeding ground for anxiety, a feeling I'd never really felt before. It was like being forced to wear an itchy coat that was one size too small. The only thing that made me feel any better was food. So I waited for lunchtime with the longing of a war bride waiting for the mail. And when it would come, I couldn't eat enough. Even after a whole deli sandwich and a bag of chips, the empty panic remained. I'd always need to go back to the snack bar for one more thing. But sometimes, I'd run out of money. And that's when the borrowing habit began. The first time I did it, it was casual and conversational. I didn't have any money on me and I knew we'd just be standing around on that slanted playground for another half hour, so I turned to Hannah and asked if I could have some money to get a candy bar. When she said no, I just asked the girl standing next to her. That girl opened her hand. She had thirty-five cents right there. I took it and never looked back. After that, borrowing got easier the more I did it. Up until that one fateful lunchtime, when Daisy Todd said no.

Daisy was mousy and odd, one of those girls who continued to intensely and publicly like horses long after the rest of us had been shamed out of it by older sisters or each other. She was the type of kid you didn't really notice, but when you did, you saw that she always walked on her tiptoes and her voice shook when she read aloud in class. She was also the kind of girl who seemed like she might start crying at any moment, which was definitely a huge liability in junior high. Unless you were trying to mooch money off her. Then it was the perfect asset.

So I didn't give it a second thought that day I walked up to her as she sat on the far end of the bench among her friends, and I asked her for a quarter. Maybe in my mind I thought she'd already lent me money, like it was our tradition; or more like I was a fun waitress and it would be a tip she wanted to give me just for swinging by and acknowledging her existence. That's why it was so very surprising when she looked me right in the eye and said no. She didn't just say no, she repeated exactly the question I'd asked her, but with a no at the top. "No, Karen, you cannot borrow thirty-five cents from me for just a second." Except instead of giving it the casual, friendly tone I'd been using, she said it with the same intensity and tone that one usually reserves for saying, "I hate your guts." Here I was, borderline popular and generously pretending to have some sort of social connection with her in exchange for money while she, quiet and mousy, was negating my improvisation. This wasn't the part she was supposed to play. Suddenly, I didn't recognize her. This was not a girl on the verge of tears. This was a girl who was mouthing off to me in front of all her friends. I was immediately horrified, but somewhere inside, I also kind of respected it. At least she wasn't crying. I made a lame joke about her being scary and started to walk away. But then she said, "Maybe you don't need any more candy." And then all the girls sitting around her laughed behind their hands, eyes wide with delight.

I was the subject of some kind of a coup. Daisy was going rogue. She was speaking for all the mousy girls around her, for mousy girls everywhere! They lent me money because they thought I'd be their friend, but it was clear I wasn't. And they'd had enough.

I didn't borrow money anymore after that. Well, not from them.

But as hurtful as that experience was, it was just a drop in the bucket compared to how awful things would eventually become in junior high. Being a thirteen-year-old girl is simply the worst experience you can have in life, including all cancers and bear attacks. It is a daily series of betrayals and base humiliations that you must figure out a way to look cute during. It's like, what the fuck.

The Daisy Uprising was my entrée into the realm of personality politics. I pretended to like Daisy and her plastic horse friends so that I could have candy whenever I wanted. But they weren't stupid. In fact, most of them were the smartest girls in the class. And as trapped as they felt in the weird bog of junior high socializing, they knew I wasn't a heavy hitter. I couldn't end them like Carmen Renata could. That Carmen was genuinely frightening. In fact, without being stunningly beautiful or their little sister, our setup wasn't meant to last.

I said this before when we talked about cults, but junior high is where I learned it first: everyone has an agenda. The horse girls wanted to be included, and they thought giving me money meant I would include them. When they realized that I only talked to them when I wanted something, they were like, "Fuck her bullshit." And honestly, it must've felt great for Daisy, finally being the one saying the mean thing instead of having the mean thing said to her. She got to flex and feel her own power. She got to set a boundary.

And she was right to. Because the harsh junior high truth is, I didn't like Daisy. Or more accurately, I had no interest in getting to know her. I didn't have any patience for the mousy girls. They brought their fear of growing up to school and paraded it around like one of those plastic horses the rest of us felt forced to put away. When I turned thirteen, the world flipped over into a frightening battleground, and girls like her put a target on my back. There was no room for generosity or pity. This was junior high.

For girls, junior high is a daily dystopian nightmare of apocalyptic emotional warfare. Kill or be killed. Gossip or be gossiped about. Figure out some way to be popular or prepare to have your body roasted on a spit on the side of the road. This metaphor is not an exaggeration. For girls in junior high, life gets REAL dark. Like, Cormac McCarthy dark. And you're only thirteen, so it's hard.

One time in Chicago, I went to a lecture series with my friend Christen, where they had a bunch of people give five-minute talks on something they loved and/or wanted other people to know about. One presenter did a talk on lightning photography. Another talked about volunteering for Habitat for Humanity. And then near the end, this lady got up and said she was going to give a speech in defense of thirteen-year-olds. The second she said that, I started crying. When has anyone in this world defended thirteen-year-olds? They're the absolute worst, and everyone agrees. They're rude and sullen and bitchy and no fun. They think they know everything, but they actually don't know anything at all, which is very embarrassing and painful to be near.

But this lady was explaining why being that age is the hardest age you ever have to be because of all the chemicals and hormones constantly raging through your body at the same time. It's like you're being drugged and then woken up with speed on a daily basis. Plus, your skin and hair and privates are all changing and you start to smell and you're suddenly aware of every pore on your face. Meanwhile, all social structure implodes and resets in a totally unfamiliar way. She pointed out how you're simultaneously the oldest version of a child and the youngest version of an adult, so you don't belong anywhere. And the only people who truly understand you are going through the same thing, so as much as they empathize, they can't connect with you because they're dealing with all the same horror you're going through plus whatever personal curveballs adolescence might be throwing them. So it's very lonely. You're not cute anymore. Everyone criticizes you. You don't get babied, and you don't get respect.

I wish I could show you a video of the level of ugly crying I was doing by the end of this speech. Her explanation forced me to face how the pain and trauma I felt being thirteen injured me fundamentally and in a way that I'd never acknowledged. So it was like a fractured feelings bone that set wrong, causing me to have a severe emotional limp and constant interpersonal relationship arthritis for the rest of my days.

Being thirteen was incredibly intense and mortifying and, at times, seemingly life-threatening. Almost every girl in seventh grade was trying as hard as she could to seem older, smarter, and more streetwise than she actually was. Being at school was a sort of dress rehearsal for being a real teenager. But Daisy and her kind were constantly blowing our cover, proudly displaying how young and dumb we actually were. They talked about stickers. They tattled. They cried at their desks. They kept insisting their classmates give a shit about their feelings. It brought out the mercilessness in all of us. It made us all want to scream, "Those days are over, you dumb babies!"

Now, society has made some nice strides in the last decade or two when it comes to bullying and feelings and respect for others, which I think is a true sign of the human race evolving. But let me explain to you how NOT like that it was in the early '80s.

Where I'm from, there were almost no parents around anywhere ever. It was straight-up *Peanuts* country. Packs of wild children routinely being dropped off at arcades or pizza parlors for hours at a time. Boys walking around with balled-up fists, ready to defend their allowance against scary older boys on too-small bikes. Girls circled up in corners, arms crossed and glaring. If you ran into trouble, whether it was a stolen quarter or a broken femur, it was yours to handle. And of course! Who better than you, with your bizarre child logic and a total inability to see the bigger picture.

Also, back then, no one's mom would come pick you up early just because, for example, you got locked out of the roller rink after accidentally skating out a side door. Too bad, so sad. You were on your own now, surviving by your wits in the parking lot while everyone you knew ate roller rink nachos inside. *So what,* you'd say to yourself. *I hate them all, anyway. The parking lot is better. It's so windy and quiet. And the pavement has a layer of gravel so I can't skate on it no matter how hard I try. This is perfect,* you'd yell aloud, since there was no one around to hear you for miles. *Another chance for me to adapt.*

You'd look around at your new environment and think, *Maybe I should go down and explore that creek bed. It's perfect! All dark and obscured by trees, littered with empty Löwenbräu cans and ominous shreds of clothing. Who knows what fascinating creek folk are waiting to meet me down there?!* But then you got a weird feeling about the creek, the way that one bush shakes as you skate-walk toward it. So you come up with an alternate plan. You decide to squat between two cars for the rest of the skating session, and if an adult walks by and asks what you're doing, you'll say you're looking for your scarf. "Really?" they'll say. "It's July." And then, you'll say—well, actually, then you'll just start crying because it'd already been twenty-five minutes of parking lot life and you simply cannot take one more second of it. Just then, everyone runs outside, and the mom of the girl who invited you pulls up and immediately starts yelling at you for wandering around the parking lot alone before pickup time in rented skates. That's what being a kid in the '80s was like in a nutshell. You were always one unalarmed emergency door away from disappearing forever.

And just for the record, no one's mom did their homework for them in the '80s. Ever. Everyone's project sucked, and the embarrassment of it sucking either made you do a better project next time or set you on the path of not caring about sucking. And as goes Ohio, so goes the nation. That's right. Junior high is when it's officially decided whether you're going to rule or suck forever. No pressure.

Oh, and there was the extra layer of horror for '80s kids: you had to be a *preppie.* That trend hit hard and fast. It made no real sense to me, as I'd had no experience with Ivy League comedy magazines or the Hamptons. Yet suddenly, all of America was supposed to dress and talk like we were the 1 percent. And that's when most of us realized that our parents didn't make enough money for us to be preppies. I can't tell you how jarring it was to wake up one day in a small farm town only to learn that my parents didn't own enough boats. And to feel real shame because of it. The preppy trend caused a massive materialistic panic and a total rearrangement of the social order at our school. Suddenly, it wasn't just the prettiest girl, but the prettiest girl with the freshest IZOD shirt who ran the game.

This was a real hard left turn from the Montessori, hippie-vibed, carob-drenched '70s we'd grown up in. Life was no longer about being kind to your neighbor and not littering and natural fibers. Suddenly, you needed boat shoes and a plaid skirt and a membership to a racquetball club. Everything became pastel sweaters and Sperry Top-Siders and headbands in short hair.

And then, on top of the pressure to be rich, everyone's parents got divorced all at once. It was right around the time MTV premiered. Suddenly, if your dad didn't make six figures on Wall Street and divorce your mom for a girl in your class, you were NO ONE. The coolest thing you could do was go to live with one parent in LA for the summer and come back wearing board shorts and a hardened stare. You'd been to that mall from the "Valley Girl" song. You made out with a skateboarder. You'd seen some shit.

My mom and her friends spent a lot of time consoling the newly separated wives. They'd meet up at one house after work, and while all the moms talked in hushed tones in the kitchen, eight to ten kids lay in mesmerized silence around the TV room watching J. J. Jackson introduce Tina Turner videos. We did that all afternoon, until the sun set and then well into the night. There was a distant cackling about "that bastard" and his "midlife crisis" in the background while Billy Idol snarled and punched the air in the foreground. There was a lot of coping with either wine or

Doritos, depending on which room you were in. As bad as the divorce epidemic was, I do have to say that I was incredibly jealous of the children of divorce. They were the least tended to of all the great abandoned masses of '80s children. They ate those chips until they barfed, and then when their mom said it was time for dinner, they'd scream, "No!" and slam their bedroom door. It was breathtaking. In my house, you'd be dead and buried for that behavior. But all divorced moms did was sigh, light another Virginia Slim, and stare out the kitchen window.

Well after dark, as we'd drive home, my mom would tell me about these women she knew who were divorcing their husbands but had never had a job or a bank account of their own. "She's never written a check!" my mom would yell, steering our silver Volvo through the pitch-black country roads. "She's never been on her own in her entire adult life! She doesn't even know who she is." I'd roll my eyes and say, "Typical," because I like to be involved. But now I see my mom was trying to teach me the value of being independent, financially and emotionally. She was saying, start developing this sense of independence now so that when you're an adult, it won't be some life-shattering adjustment.

Let's skip now to the mid-2000s so I can tell you about a thing that happened that ties all this shit together. My life had very suddenly become the thing I dreamed it would be. I was a writer for a daily TV show, which meant I had a career and consistent money. These were things I never truly thought I'd have, what with my alcoholism and repeated failures in other attempted careers. (Fuck you, the Gap. You didn't fire me, I quit.)

So during the third season of this show, at Christmastime, I drove onto the lot and went to pull into my parking space, when I saw there was already a car in it. It was a silver BMW with a big red bow around the hood just like a car commercial. It took me a minute to realize it was a present for me. My boss wanted to show their appreciation for the work I'd done, so they bought me a car. A BMW, to be precise. I'd never wanted a BMW per se, but I also never thought I could have one. Suddenly, I felt like I'd truly made it in Hollywood. My proof was right there in front of me wrapped in a ridiculously big ribbon.

If you drive a fancy car in LA, it either means you're successful or you're leasing a car to seem successful. Either way, it brings the driver a strange kind of status. Suddenly, I was pulling up to valets and feeling kinda proud. I felt rich. I felt like I belonged. I felt like . . . *a preppie.* (See? That's me wrapping things up in a metaphorical bow for your reading pleasure. I told you I would, and then I did.) I could not believe that the impossible had finally happened. I looked like one of those people whose parents had boat money and then got divorced and then bought them an apology pony. I was now of the LA elite. But the car was subtly changing me. I started turning left on a yellow light even though I was the third car. I went 110 on the freeway when I had nowhere to be. I developed a disdain for slow cars, shitty-looking cars, cars with more than one bumper sticker. I blasted my German stereo and gunned my Nazi engine. It wasn't my problem. It had been given to me. I had no choice but to become a douche. I was killing it in the business. That was the Hollywood way. This car meant I was better than other people.

A year later, that job ended abruptly. I was totally disillusioned about who I'd become and what I thought I knew. I'd spent five years of my life at that show, given up performing comedy, abandoned friendships, and missed family functions. And here I was at the end, wondering if it'd been worth it. Of course, it feels good to be successful, especially if you've never felt anything like it before. And having money rules. But we all believe money and status will change us for the better. You lose yourself in the trappings of success: luxury cars, designer shoes, cashmere sweaters in every color. They're all just props and costumes that our inner thirteen-year-old thinks we need to survive on the slanted, gravel-covered playground of adulthood. I had to go through this huge life trauma to realize that I never cared about being a preppie when I was thirteen. I just wanted to stop suffering so fucking much.

I sold the BMW a week after I left that job. I didn't like the way it made me feel.

Buy Your Own Shit: Final Thoughts

GEORGIA: We've all known people who don't think they should have to "buy their own stuff." What are some characteristics of those people?

KAREN: Having grown up as one of those people, I'd say it happens when you grow up never having to provide for yourself. It makes you think the world somehow owes you, and it makes you resent hard work. But then hopefully, you meet people who have worked hard all their lives, and you get some perspective and you learn the value of contributing something and being of use, and it makes you see things differently.

GEORGIA: What was a time in your life that something ended up being too good to be true?

KAREN: Remember when everyone thought New York Seltzer was no-calorie when it came out because it had *seltzer* in the name? It was the '80s, and we were very naïve. We drank SO much New York Seltzer, we thought it was the answer to our diet prayers.

GEORGIA: What's the first thing that you remember ever buying for yourself?

KAREN: A Kristy and Jimmy McNichol record at the Music Coop record store in Petaluma. I loved her on the show *Family.* It was an incredible album. I consider it their *Dark Side of the Moon.*

GEORGIA: What's the last really big purchase you made? How did it make you feel?

KAREN: I got a new car last year, and it was a huge relief. I didn't buy one for a while because I was afraid to spend too much and get into more financial trouble, so I kept waiting and not buying one and taking Ubers everywhere. I inhaled SO much cologne. And then, when I knew we were going to be making a steady income from this podcast, I got the car I wanted and not the car I knew I could afford. It was a great big symbol for coming out of my financial crisis, and that makes me smile every time I get into it.

STAY OUT OF THE FOREST

SSDGM

art by Lucie Rice Illustration & Design

8

STAY OUT OF THE FOREST

KAREN: "Stay out of the forest" was the last step in my aforementioned three-part process to ensuring personal safety. Nothing good happens in a forest. Ask Hansel, Gretel, or Harry Potter. But we all know that avoiding an entire land feature won't guarantee nothing bad will ever happen to us. For this life is filled with conceptual forests that we'd do best to stay away from as well. So, gather 'round the campfire, children. It's scary story time.

Georgia Loses Her Brother but Finds Herself

There's a giant tapestry covering one wall in the podcast loft, the open upstairs room in my apartment where we used to record the podcast and have all of our fan art. It's just a huge photo of a beautiful, bucolic forest with nothing but pine trees and rivers for miles and miles. Most people would look at that tapestry and feel a sense of relaxation and ease; maybe they'd use it to help with meditation or put it across from their bed to stare at when falling asleep at night, but I—and I'm sure a lot of Murderinos can relate—can't look at it without wondering about the dead bodies. I look at that thing and just think there have to be dead bodies hidden underneath the canopy of trees or buried deep beneath the soil of the forest floor.

How do you find a body in the woods? No, seriously. How does any-one ever even start looking for a body in the woods?! It's *the woods*. And the woods are *vast as fuck*. Everything is covered in trees! And there are freaking bears! And whatever bramble is! It makes no sense to me, and then I think of all the bodies that will never be found because of the pure vastness and all-encompassing hugeness of the forest, and it gives me a tiny panic attack.

When I was a little kid, I thought it would be so cool to find a dead body. Once again, I blame Stephen King for this, along with my over-active imagination, as watching *Stand by Me* as a six-year-old gave me some crazy ideas about what an adventure finding a body would be. And also I associated River Phoenix and his all-encompassing gorgeousness with finding a body, so that didn't help.

My dad used to take me and my older siblings, Asher and Leah, on camping trips every summer since before I can remember. So I've been thinking about bodies in woods since . . . before I can remember. Dad had custody of us every other weekend and for two weeks every summer. Instead of bingeing TV and complaining about how hot it was in his small apartment in a complex that seemed made specifically for divorcés, he'd plan a big road trip to a national forest for a week of camping and hiking and complaining about how hot it was in nature. The whole point of these trips was some kind of personality-building exercise that only made sense to my dad. He wanted to instill in us self-sufficiency, a work ethic, and probably survival skills for when the end days come? I don't really know. MARTY?!

When times were good, he'd pick us up in a big RV. When things were just OK, he'd pick us up in a smaller camper. When he pulled up in his beat-up minivan, we knew not to even *ask* to go into souvenir shops. But whatever he pulled up in, Asher, Leah, and I would sprint to the curb and scream: "I'M IN THE FRONT NO TRADE-BACKS!"* Because that's how you won the coveted front seat in the Hardstark households. Don't ask questions or meaning. It was just Sibling Law.

We'd drive forever, and I'm not bratty-little-are-we-there-yet-kid exaggerating. We'd actually drive ten-plus hours in one day, partially because of the distance we needed to cover and partially because my dad drives like an old man (Marty! I'm sorry, but it's TRUE!). He'd only bring two cassettes to listen to as we drove: Paul Simon's *Graceland*, which I now know every single word to and the title song of which we danced our father/daughter dance to at my wedding, and a tape of bagpipe music. Who the hell listens to bagpipe music?? With kids???

---

* See pg 271.

And we really did listen to it whenever we got sick of Paul Simon's voice, that or the shitty AM radio station of whatever small town we were driving through.

We never stopped for food, as my dad was both frugal and strict with the allotment of stops we took. Instead, he'd have the dreaded small cooler in the car with the GROSSEST healthy snacks, like peanuts and raisins that were in two separate containers so we would have to pour a little of each into our dirty hands to combine them and make something resembling trail mix. Juice boxes, grapes, and stale pretzels rounded out the lackluster snack food department. Oh, the unhealthy snacks we coveted from the gas stations we'd stop at. Chips and hot dogs that had been sitting in the warmer for hours on end and oh my gosh LUNCHABLES. I still love shitty gas station food as an adult probably because I was never allowed to have it as a kid. On the few occasions when we *would* stop to grab food to go, it would be with the stern warning to "eat over your clothes" lest we make a mess in the car.*

Now listen, one of the reasons I don't want kids is because my siblings and I were the biggest monsters ever. I'm talking constant drama

---

*   See pg 271.

and turmoil. Love and hate and betrayal and laughter and a little ADHD (thanks to yours truly) thrown in for good measure. How did my parents not murder us?? We didn't have a token troublemaker kid in my family. All three of us were constantly getting into trouble—at school, at home, in Target, wherever. I once told my soccer coach to go fuck himself when he wouldn't stop hounding me. I think I was ten. And we were all like that. (One time, Asher locked Leah and me in our bedroom with an intricate mechanism made out of yarn and wouldn't let us out until we drank an orange juice / raw egg concoction. We were in there for three hours before we relented and drank it. And the only person who's ever punched me in the stomach is my sister. Twice. I got her back by throwing a Barbie at her head.)

One of my favorite family stories is when Asher's teacher made him write "I will not wipe my Kleenex on someone else's property" a hundred times in his notebook after a kid complained about Asher's gross antics. We still have that piece of paper framed somewhere in our family.

Sometimes, when Dad just couldn't take us anymore, he'd start repeating the phrase "Move away from me now, move away from me now."* You knew he was serious because he said it in this creepy monotone that left no room for discussion. You moved away from him. Now.

After hours upon hours of driving, we'd reach our campground as dusk was falling, and we'd all pile out and stretch loudly and gratefully. While the journey sucked, the destination made it almost worth it. The smell of the forest, the pine trees and faint whiffs of the first campfires being lit, the seclusion and wildness of it all—especially after having spent the previous year in my hometown planned community that didn't have a single tree that wasn't planted without strict planning and not a weed in sight—hit my child brain with a little bit of awe. And I could sense something in my dad change, too. It was

* See pg 271.

like I could see him morph from a suburban soccer dad with responsibilities who wore a fanny pack and lived in an all-off-white one-bedroom apartment into a kinda feral mountain man who could whittle things and lived off the land . . . and still wore a fanny pack.

The first step to our camping experience was always to erect the tent. Sounds easy, right? No. It is not. It is stupid and I hate it. First of all, Dad's tent was at least twenty years old. None of those modern tent luxuries like taking less than an hour to put up and not needing to forage for big rocks to hold down an even more ancient blue tarp. This pole went here maybe, that snap went there or there or there, cue one of the four of us throwing a tantrum and stomping into the forest to cry and scream our frustrations into the wilderness. The woods are a good place to scream in frustration. They've heard the frustrated screams of enraged family members since humans first existed, and they don't judge or tell you that *you* were the one being a dick; they accept and envelop your screams and use the excess carbon dioxide you emit to grow. Everyone needs a little scream in the woods sometimes.

Plus, kids wandering off alone into the wilderness—or anywhere, for that matter—was an OK thing back in the '80s and '90s. Kids were free to go off on their own into places like the fucking forest. Yes, small child. Go take a walk. Kids were expected to go figure their shit out and compose themselves. When they were ready to stop being an asshole, they could join the family again. I can't tell you how many times I got lost in a forest as a kid because I was fed up with my sister or dad and decided to run away and live a life on the road or maybe make friends with Bigfoot or something.

Eventually, I'd wander back in the gathering darkness, a little scared of what might be lurking in the inky night or watching me from behind a tree or camouflaged in the tree canopy, but also lured by the smell of my dad's insanely delicious barbecued chicken cooking on the grill. The recipe is incredibly complicated and has been in our family for generations, but I've decided to share it with you now.

Marty's Famous Barbecued Chicken

    4 boneless, skinless chicken breasts (or whatever chicken part is on sale that day)

    1 jar of generic-brand barbeque sauce

    1 large plastic generic-brand ziplock bag

·   Put chicken parts in the bag. Pour entire jar of barbecue sauce into the bag. Put bag into the dreaded cooler alongside the juice boxes and grapes for the 10+ hours you're driving to the campsite. Cook over an open fire or small charcoal grill and hope that you don't give your children salmonella, but if you do, it'll probably give them character, so don't worry about it too much. When your daughter asks for the recipe as an adult, break her heart by telling her it was just cheap chicken parts and jarred barbeque sauce.

After dinner, my dad would let my brother light a bonfire even though my brother should in no way have been allowed to play with fire, and everyone would chill with a book or play poker until we got tired, and we'd all crawl into our scratchy hand-me-down sleeping bags side by side in the tent that claimed to be a four-person tent. The foresty sounds of the forest and the crackle of the bonfire slowly dying lulling us to sleep. The animals and serial killers tucking in for the night nearby.

I was seven the summer we went to the Grand Canyon. One evening, after a long day of adventuring, collecting rocks, and heat stroke, Asher had yet to get back from a solo hike and it was starting to get dark. He was about ten years old, a scrawny kid who had trouble in school because he was so smart he was bored, so he found other ways to entertain himself that usually involved him annoying someone and getting sent to the principal's office (see Kleenex story above).

So it was dark, he was gone, and as much as I always swore that

I hated him and wished he wasn't my brother, I started freaking the fuck out a little, convinced that my big brother was dead, eaten by a mountain lion or hacked to death by an ax murderer.

I was sitting close to the fire, my knees turning red from the heat of the flames, and I kept looking over my shoulder expectantly into the dark woods that butted up against our camp. I finally dog-eared the page I'd been staring at for twenty minutes but not actually reading. Leah was fidgeting with the hair wrap that she'd paid a local to braid into a lock of her hair earlier that day, trying to pretend she didn't give a shit, but she kept looking toward the woods Asher should have walked out of by now, too.

"Shouldn't he be back by now?" I asked, my voice not much louder than the crackle of the fire.

No one responded.

My dad didn't seem worried, despite the fact that he was a champion worrier. After a decade of parenting a hyperactive kid like my bro, I guess sometimes you forget that the bad things that can befall your wild kid aren't *just* those things *caused* by that kid. Ya know?

As I was just starting to learn from shows like *Unsolved Mysteries,* pics of missing kids on the back of milk cartons, and the death of my long-time school crush David R., who died suddenly that previous year of leukemia, bad things befell people all the fucking time.

The first time I heard about NecroSearch was through an introduction to what is now one of my "favorite" murders—as in the one that's broken my heart the most and that I'm sure will be in my mind and heart for the rest of my life*—that of Michele Wallace. NecroSearch is an incredible organization made up of "scientists, specialists, and behaviorists, who use the latest technology and the most advanced

---

*   I just googled "NecroSearch Michele Wallace," and a *My Favorite Murder* fan site was the second link that popped up. I am just so amazed that I get to be associated with such an amazing organization in this way. Life is CRAZY!

techniques to help solve 'unsolvable' crimes" and "provide assistance to law enforcement agencies in the search for and recovery of human remains" (aka a bunch of crazy-smart people who go to extreme lengths to help find bodies hidden in fucking forests and other insane places. I HIGHLY recommend *No Stone Unturned: The True Story of the World's Premier Forensic Investigators* by Steve Jackson).

It was an old episode of one of my favorite shows, *Cold Case Files*, where I learned about Michele and everything about her death stayed with me. Sweet baby angel Michele was a beautiful person—she was outgoing and ambitious, and had she not been murdered by the fucking trash-monster Roy Melanson during a solo camping trip in 1974 in the Rocky Mountains (accompanied by her trusty dog, Okie), there's no telling what kind of positive mark she could have left on the world. Instead, she changed the face of cold cases forever. Twelve years after her scalp was found with the attached hair still in their signature braids (OMFG) on a trail in the same general area it was thought she had picked up a hitchhiking Melanson (who, unbeknownst to her, was a convicted rapist and also the fucking spawn of Satan), the NecroSearch team was able to find what remained of her skeleton using, among other fascinating techniques, forensic analysis of the leaves found on the scalp and hair, which lead them to where her body would most likely have been left. Prosecutors, who previously were worried about taking Melanson to trial without a body, despite a mountain of evidence proving his guilt, were now able to take that fucker to task, and he was found guilty and sentenced to life in prison, where I hope he got beat up a lot.

This case not only started my fascination with cold cases but also marked the time in my life where there was no chance in fucking hell I was going camping or hiking in the forest ever again.

That night when Asher disappeared, I was inconsolable. In my little seven-year-old mind, we were in a state of emergency, and the helplessness I felt that we couldn't do anything to help find my brother made me feel like I was going to burst out of my own skin. I also wondered if this meant that, should I go missing one day, no one would bother looking for me either, and as someone who already had a deep fear of being kidnapped, this scared me almost as much as the actual kidnapping did. It was up to me to sound the alarms at my brother's absence, just as I hoped he would do for me if I ever went missing. Looking back, I think that my reaction probably made a little more sense than my dad's calmness did, but hey, I'm not trying to tell him how to parent (yes, I am). In reality, knowing my dad and his deep-seated need for a sense of order and control, the eating over your clothes in the car and our immaculate campsite presented as proof, he probably *was* freaking out; he just didn't want to show me and Leah and worry us even more.

It was well past our normal bedtime when we finally had no choice but to lie down and try to fall asleep, and Asher still hadn't come back. I could picture the feature on *Unsolved Mysteries,* the incredibly creepy intro music playing as Robert Stack described the eerie circumstances of Asher's disappearance in his gravelly voice, telling viewers that perhaps *they* had a clue to unlock the mystery of his whereabouts. I'd always wanted to be the viewer that had the clue to unlock one of the mysteries, and now I would actually be on the side that *needed* a clue, begging the audience for information that led to the answer of my missing brother. Leah and my dad and mom would be there, too. I'd wear the blue dress with the big pockets that I wore the first day of school, and my tears would bring the nation to its knees . . . OK, to be honest, the prospect of being on TV might have gotten me just a little excited, but the excitement passed another two hours later when he still hadn't come back.

What I also learned from the Michele Wallace case for the first time in my true crime–obsessed history was that these cases weren't just about the victim and murderer, the police and detectives, and the men and women who (hopefully) brought the bad guy to justice. That if

I were going to delve into this with such gusto, I also needed to think about the victims in the periphery—about the lives that go on after the case is closed and the killer has been (hopefully) locked away—the victim's family and friends whose lives are forever, irrevocably changed.

You see, two weeks after Michele went missing, before there was even evidence that she met with foul play, or that she hadn't just extended her camping trip, Michele's mother killed herself. She knew that not hearing from her beloved daughter for even a couple of days meant that the worst had happened, and she couldn't even wait to find out if her fears were valid. She just knew, and she also knew that she couldn't handle a life without Michele. My heart broke for that woman, as well as Michele's father and brother, who had to stay behind and live in this awful world where awful people like Roy Melanson would be allowed to go free for decades, to kill again during that time, and that these peripheral victims were powerless. I love staying up late into the night and watching or reading about real-life stories of the extremes of humanity and the evil that lurks in the real world. Those stories help me process my own fears and anxieties around death, but I have an obligation as an avid participant in true crime to remember that many people have to live in those stories, and it's more to them than just a cautionary tale or a late-night thrill.

I didn't think I'd sleep with Asher still gone, but I must have dozed off a bit because shortly after the fire had burned its final ember, I heard footsteps crunching across the otherwise silent campground followed by the zipper on our tent being pulled and a swish as the door flap was pushed aside, then the sound of Asher slipping into his sleeping bag. I was so relieved! And so pissed! We were all awake in an instant, reprimanding him for being gone so long.

"Asher! Where the hell were you?! I seriously thought you were DEAD!"

He casually told us he'd wandered off the trail and gotten lost. "But

I found a hiking group, and they led me back to camp," he said, changing into his PJs inside his sleeping bag and then resting his dumb big-brother head on his Star Wars pillowcase.

I think that was the moment I realized that I actually did love my gross, annoying, embarrassing, asshole of an older brother even though he once threw an open carton of applesauce at my face and his nickname for me was simply "bitch." I wanted him to leave me alone, but I didn't want him to be kidnapped by a family of bears or fall off a cliff!

A few years later, Asher (still not dead or living with bears) and Leah (who had discovered boys and lost interest in being my friend) went off to high school. I was almost out of junior high, and my dad couldn't have *paid* us to stay the night at his divorced-dad apartment every other weekend, let alone go camping with him. Asher was going to GWAR and Primus concerts on the weekends, and Leah was deep into an unhealthy high school relationship, and the "four-person" tent could barely hold two of us by then.

In late summer 1994, I was fourteen, and when my dad pulled his beat-up minivan to the curb outside Mom's place, I didn't have to invoke Sibling Law to get the front seat—it was just Dad and me. Although I had adamantly refused to camp deep into the forest, having been traumatized by it from more years of those summer trips than I could count by then, I did agree to go camping on a beach, which sounded exotic and relaxing. We drove at my dad's usual pace of six-plus hours on what should have been a three-hour drive down the California coast and across the border to a little campground on a beach in Mexico that felt less like a tropical beach and more like a postapocalyptic hobo camp with its beat-up trailers and pup tents and feral children running around clothed in the sickly greenish foam of the surf.

All the camping tourists looked like they had come into Mexico to outrun something, possibly someone trying to cash in on a loan or from a warrant. We set up the tent with the sweltering heat of the sun beating down on us and on the hard-packed sand, and as my dad warned me not to open my mouth in the water, I was already daydreaming of an air-conditioned hotel room and sitting poolside. But it also just wasn't the same without Asher and Leah there to drive us both crazy. After one night, we packed up and headed out for home early.

We finished packing all our sand-covered gear into the minivan, and Dad steered around a pack of children as we headed out of the parking lot and toward the main highway that would lead us to the hours-long line of cars waiting to cross the border back into the U.S. That's when lights flashed behind us, and the loud *whoop* of a police siren alerted us to pull the car over onto the shoulder of the crumbling street.

"Be cool," my dad joked through the tension as he pumped the manual handle to roll down his window and the police approached. A quick conversation ensued in stilted Spanish between my dad and the scowling cop, after which he turned briskly back to his squad car, and my dad, rolling his window back up, informed me that we were ordered to follow the squad car back to the police station for reasons that hadn't been given to my dad, aside from telling him that he had run a stop sign that we were both sure didn't actually exist. His always-composed, control-freak voice had a detectable hint of nervousness, which put me into full-on panic mode.

At the station, my dad gave me strict orders to stay in the locked car while he went inside. He assured me that he just had to give them a little money and we would be fine, but he also warned me not to unlock the door under any circumstances. He'd recently told me of a high school friend of his who had just gotten out of a Thai prison after decades of harsh imprisonment over a possibly trumped-up drug charge and the mental havoc it had wreaked upon his life. So, convinced my dad was off to meet a similar fate, I was almost in tears as I watched him walk into the police station.

The minivan became a sweatbox in less than a minute, but I didn't dare roll down the window even an inch. Sweat beaded on my forehead and inside my training bra as I waited for what felt like hours but was probably twenty minutes before my dad came back and we drove the fuck away. Relief and fresh, glorious wind from the open window washed over me as we booked it for the border and he told me what had happened inside the police station. The police had indeed wanted money, a lot of money, for the alleged driving infraction. In a move that took a huge amount of chutzpah, my father refused. Instead, he told them he'd give them a smaller amount of money to put toward their widows' funds, donations given to the wives of fallen officers, but that his own father had been on the police force in Los Angeles and that if they didn't let us go, my dad would make a phone call to the LAPD and there'd be hell to pay.

After making him wait, the officers agreed to the smaller sum, and my father, his wallet a little lighter, was free to go.

Here's the thing: my dad's father had been a barber who lost all his money betting on horse racing. My dad had been bullshitting on a level I didn't even know he was capable of. I sat proud and stunned in the passenger seat as we waited in the long line to get through the border crossing into the U.S.

A short time later, on a Friday night out with some friends and acquaintances, I was given a hit of LSD and took it without a second thought. I ended up staying out all night with these friends, crashing early in the morning atop some dirty blankets on the floor of some squatter compound as my high slowly wore off into some trippy-dreamed dozing. I hadn't called home to let my mom know I'd be gone all night, figuring that her casual latchkey parenting didn't necessitate such formal practices, even at my young age of fourteen. But apparently I was wrong. Because she called my dad, who called the cops, who of course wouldn't let him report me as a missing person that early in my disappearance, but nevertheless, all parties were concerned about the whereabouts of a fourteen-year-old kid who was freshly out of rehab and prone to bad decisions.

When I finally called home the next morning from a pay phone outside of a local liquor store that sold single cigarettes for a quarter, I could tell I was in deep trouble merely by the angry way in which my mom answered the phone. I headed straight home and was grounded for the rest of the weekend, which was fine with me, as I wanted nothing more than to sleep my drug hangover away forever.

By this point, Asher had moved in with my dad to a somewhat larger divorcé apartment because the tension between my brother and mother had gotten so volatile as he went through puberty that there were holes kicked in walls (him) and threats of taking a hammer to his precious pre-internet computer (her).

When I saw my brother later that week, Asher got serious with me, which isn't something he's prone to do. Normally, we didn't discuss either of our bad behavior, allowing the other the room to fuck up without judgment. It was a nice unspoken understanding we had come to. While our parents and teachers and school and society and therapists constantly scrutinized our behavior, I could count on my brother not making me hate myself even more than I already did by bringing up all my shortcomings, and vice versa. There were no lectures, no shaming, and no analyzing.

So when he let out a deep, world-weary sigh and couldn't make eye contact with me, I knew something was up.

"Georgia, the night you disappeared, I heard Dad in his room, through the door," he told me. "He was sobbing and praying. He thought you were dead."

I've never felt like such a monster in my life. I could handle anger and yelling from my mom. Hell, I'd been handling it ever since my dad left home. But aside from a clenched-teethed "Move away from me now," my dad had never shown anger or disappointment. He'd only ever been patient and supportive. This is someone who has never ended a phone call with me without telling me how proud he is of me, even through some bad shit when there was no reason for anyone to be proud of me. So knowing I made him sob hurt my heart in a way I wasn't ready for. And it made me think about what would have happened if I actually hadn't, or couldn't, come home the next morning.

I've lived my life since then with the image of my dad in the back of my mind and how he'd react if some dumb decision or blasé attitude toward life led to me dying or being killed. Being his clear favorite child (sorry, Asher and Leah, but you KNOW this is true! I mean, how could it not be? I'm kind of the awesomest), I'm pretty sure it would not be something he'd ever be able to recover from. And OK, fine, also if his two less favorite children met the same fate. So I'm a little extra careful, a little less of a risk taker, a little less of a forest-goer because of that.

So be adventurous and take risks and go into the forest (metaphorically speaking), but please keep an eye on your surroundings. 'Cause you never know when there will be a hitchhiking rapist, a questionable stop sign, or a hiking trail that leads to death. The people who care about you won't be the same without you.*

---

*   Asher, Leah, and I still say this stuff to each other all the time. (e.g., Leah accuses me of stealing her wedges: *Move away from me now, move away from me now . . .*)

Karen's Lessons from Listeners and Canadian Aldermen

When I was growing up, there was a weekly column in the newspaper called "Hints from Heloise." This was long before the internet, back when they would print out a pile of information every day and an unattended nine-year-old boy on a bicycle would throw it at your house before dawn. People would write to Heloise with a household problem and she'd tell them how to fix it using everyday items. Gum in your kid's hair? Put peanut butter on it! Wine stain on a white shirt? Put salt on it! (Those were both off the top of my head. The wine/salt one is real, but now that I think about the peanut butter one, it might have been a prank my sister pulled on me once when I got gum in my hair.)

As a child, I read Heloise's hints with wonder. *Why aren't they teaching this in schools?* I'd think. Putting fresh peaches in a brown paper bag to speed up the ripening process should be part of the third-grade curriculum for all of North America. I mean, if I didn't know that combining vinegar and baking soda created a powerful yet organic cleanser for the kitchen sink, then how could anyone else in my class? It also made me obsess on what other great fixes I was missing out on. It seemed like no matter what the problem was, Heloise had an encyclopedic knowledge of simple solutions that were easy, convenient, and often involved butter. At the time, she also had long gray hair, so I was drawn to the whole "eye of newt, wing of bat" thing she had going on. It felt like she was sharing ancient women's knowledge that had been banned by the church, but her family had secreted away the forbidden books. I don't know, I just really liked it.

In the early days of the podcast, when Georgia and I would read the details of horrible crimes to each other, I think we felt the need to pull a useful lesson out of the senseless tragedy. I know I did. I'd think, *What can we do to make sure this never happens again? How do we identify the warning signs that the victim missed?* We thought if we identified the "big mistake" and then pointed it out, a preventative measure could be taken. In my mind, it became us giving advice, Hints from Heloise–style. The stain was always the same: being murdered. And the solutions were practical, organic, and most importantly, effective: use the buddy system, get a large dog, generally mistrust all strangers, stay out of the forest. If we just had enough tricks to share, we could help each other outsmart these predators.

And look (listen), they were good pieces of advice, but the truth is, the kind of violence we're talking about isn't some small, immaterial stain waiting to be removed with salt. And even if it were, we're no Heloise. (She's truly awesome, by the way. Aside from having a syndicated newspaper column since 1980, she's written fourteen books, and she won the National Mental Health Association's first-ever award for outstanding contribution to mental health education. And she's the one who taught me the trick of using lemon juice to fade freckles that I mentioned in an earlier chapter. Her accomplishments know no bounds.)

We've said this many times, but I'm going to repeat it here for anyone who might find it unclear: none of the advice we give in this book or have given on our podcast is qualified. We're only experts in our own experiences. We don't have college educations or training of any kind, and if either of us has ever outsmarted a serial killer, we don't know about it. What we definitely have are big old-fashioned blind spots. Which is why we've learned to be grateful when our listeners point out our mistakes and allow us to adjust. I truly hate nothing more than finding out I have no idea how much I don't know. I find it shameful to have been ignorant in the first place, and that shame makes me resistant to learning. But too bad for me and anyone like me. The only way we can evolve and grow is by accepting our flaws and doing our best to grow out of them. This podcast has been a lot like life in that way: one big, semi-involuntary learning experience.

So when multiple people pointed out that some of our safety advice could be taken as victim blaming, I was shocked and, honestly, slightly offended. I thought, *Don't you know us? We're the noblest of all creatures! We're women trying to help women stay out of trouble! We only strive to create a sisterhood of security, freedom, and confidence. Of course we're on the victim's side! Of course we don't think anyone deserves it! We're just streetwise city girls trying to lend a helping hand! Eye of newt!* There's really nothing like the self-righteousness of the partially informed.

When we were asked to listen to our own advice from the point of view of an assault survivor, we suddenly saw how our offhanded "fixes," like "Never get into a car with someone you just met," were tinged with the invisible final clause "but since you did, you're to blame for whatever happens."

We'd never thought of it that way. And the idea that anyone thought we did really sucked.

It reminds me of something I read while I was researching Paul Bernardo and his wife, Karla Homolka, the horrifying yet Canadian husband-and-wife serial-killing team some called the Ken and Barbie Killers.

That story actually starts in May 1987, when a man began attacking and raping young women in the Scarborough area of Toronto. He attacked at night around bus stops where the women had just gotten off the bus alone. The longer he eluded police, the more vicious and violent the attacks became. Over the span of one year, the Scarborough Rapist attacked seven girls. And I'm calling them *girls* because the majority of them were teenagers, some as young as fifteen years old.

When the police finally held a press conference, the message the local constable had for the women of Toronto was surprisingly callous. He actually said, out loud and for the record:

"Don't expect people to watch out for you if you happen to come back at 1:00 A.M. in the morning off the bus. It would be nice to think that you can go anywhere you like nowadays, but don't put yourself in a vulnerable position."

Riiiiight.

OK, first of all, just a general note to the constable: if you say, "1:00 A.M.," you don't also need to say, "in the morning." It's redundant and it makes you sound like a cartoon rooster with a Southern accent. Second of all, what's with that tone? The disdain and condescension coming from him here is palpable. Plus, I looked it up, and it turns out that in Canada, a constable is what we Americans call a police chief. Ergo, it was LITERALLY HIS JOB to watch out for women getting off the bus at 1:00 A.M. in the morning.

Now, as any good true-crime aficionado knows, this constable was most likely under an immense amount of pressure to catch this serial rapist. Someone was terrorizing his city in one very specific neighborhood with the exact same MO each time, and yet he and his men could not figure out how to apprehend him. The constable was probably getting yelled at by whatever a Canadian mayor is called, angry neighborhood groups were probably demanding answers at town hall meetings, reporters were probably hounding him day and night.

I'm sure that every time this man heard about a new attack, it hurt him personally. I'm sure it weighed on him and kept him awake at night. He knew every detail of every case. Every broken bone and soul and what school they went to. And no matter what he tried, it just kept happening. Chances are, he was frustrated and humiliated that he was failing so publicly at being constable. He couldn't tell the rapist to stop, so he did the only thing he could think to do: blame the victims. He chastised the women of Scarborough for assuming they had the right to move around their city in safety. It was probably much easier for him to talk about what women needed to be doing than to address the fact that he couldn't catch one extremely fucked-up guy. He was familiar with men like this rapist, more animal than human. So the constable did the only thing his panicking brain could think of: talk directly to the people this was happening to and tell them to stop "allowing" it to happen. There. That'll solve it.

Very few people understand how best to deal with this kind of violent crime and the emotional impact it has on everyone. It's a horror movie come to life. Week after week, the people of Toronto had to read about a monster in their midst that the police couldn't catch. Suddenly, everyone is vulnerable, and that creates a culture of fear. Even in police officers themselves. For them, it was probably much easier to imagine that all the young women in Toronto who were taking the bus at night were simply caricatures of the sloppy drunk girl who can't walk in her own heels and will not listen to reason. I bet it was a relief for some people to hear authorities come to this conclusion. The issue is no longer that there's a predatory psychopath in their city who's outsmarting the cops. Now the issue is young women's failings as critical thinkers.

I like to think that some mouthy broad somewhere along the line pointed out to this constable that if women in Toronto were still taking the bus late at night knowing full well that a serial rapist was on the loose, they weren't doing it for fun. The odds are very low that they were laughing in the face of danger for the adrenaline rush or the need to rebel with indignant carelessness. These were women who *had no choice* but to take the bus at night. Single mothers with two jobs and no car. Women who couldn't afford to drive. Women with DUIs. Women who were legally blind, deaf, had been in terrible car accidents and were afraid to drive. There are so many reasons why people chose to roll the personal safety dice in this situation, but the overarching theme with most of them was probably desperation and definitely need. No, the women who continued to ride the bus at night alone in Scarborough in the late '80s were most likely doing what they had to do to survive—in spite of the danger. And more importantly, *they* were not putting themselves in a vulnerable position. The *serial rapist* was making a normal position vulnerable by being a serial rapist.

Don't worry, it gets worse. Later that month, an alderman proposed an especially backward solution: a curfew for women. *A CURFEW FOR WOMEN*. This civic leader's best idea to prevent more rape was to require the half of the population, who were definitely not the perpetrators of said rapes, to remain indoors at night.

I mean, seriously. Wouldn't the logical solution be a curfew for tall, blond males between the ages of twenty-five and thirty-five matching the description of the rapist? Or a curfew for convicted sex offenders? Or a curfew for constables and aldermen with bad ideas?

His statement might as well have been, "What do women have to do at night that's so important they need to be taking the bus across town? They should just stay home with their aprons and their curlers and stop making problems for us, the busy and important men of this city." Again, I like to think there was a reporter who looked like Ruth Bader Ginsburg sitting in on that meeting who gave that guy the what for. Or maybe everyone just rolled their eyes and waited for him to stop talking like they always did. No curfew was ever enforced, as far as my paltry research tells me, so someone said something.

All of this makes me think of the story my friend Paul told me about his mom who lived in that neighborhood when the Scarborough Rapist was at large. She was in her sixties and she liked to swim laps in the rooftop pool of her apartment building for exercise. So one morning, she went up to swim some laps alone. When she got there, she had the pool all to herself. As she swam, a young man came out onto the roof deck and began to watch her. She was immediately uncomfortable. Why would this good-looking young man silently stand and stare at a woman her age that way? But she went on swimming. The young man began walking along the side of the pool with her as she swam. Now she had no doubt there was something wrong with him. Her discomfort turned into fear. She had nowhere to go. She wasn't going to get out and confront him. Her only option was to keep swimming and hope he went away. But he didn't go away. He continued to stare and stalk her from the side of the pool. Then, just as her fear began to give way to real panic, a big group of people burst out onto the roof deck, talking and laughing. Kids jumped into the pool with her as their parents settled into deck chairs. Amid all the commotion, the man disappeared.

So my friend Paul's mom got out of the pool, went back downstairs to her apartment, and, being a talented artist, drew that man's face from memory. She put the drawing into her desk drawer. When the Scarborough Rapist's arrest was finally reported on the news, her family was sitting in her living room. She saw his face on TV, gasped, and pulled out that picture she'd drawn. It was the same young man who stalked her at the pool that day.

I retold that last part in the simplest way for clarity, but the chronology is slightly different. The man who was eventually identified as the Scarborough Rapist, Paul Bernardo, was first arrested for a series of murders attributed to someone nicknamed the Schoolgirl Killer. After taking him into custody, police learned that the Schoolgirl Killer nickname was inaccurate. In a shocking series of discoveries, evidence was found proving that Bernardo's wife, Karla, had helped him lure, torture, rape, and murder all of their young victims, including her own fourteen-year-old sister. From then on, the press dubbed them the Ken and Barbie Killers. While under arrest for those crimes, police finally matched Bernardo's DNA with the Scarborough Rapist's. His capture put an end to a six-year reign of terror that escalated to some of the most depraved murders in Canadian history.

Had a woman using the pool in her own apartment building put herself in a vulnerable position by swimming in the same spot a serial rapist somehow had access to? Were her expectations of safety unreasonable? Was she any more or less innocent than the Scarborough Rapist's victims because she wasn't on a bus at 1:00 A.M. in the morning?

It's a trick. None of these questions matter. Focusing on why women have the gall to walk around in public asking for it all day long is something small minds do when finding a violent psychopath is proving difficult. And although it may bring needed relief to those battered by the day-to-day of trying to catch a serial rapist, I'd bet good money it's never helped solve a crime.

The good news is, there were some creative minds hard at work back then. Someone, and it could have been one of these same constables or aldermen mentioned above, finally had an idea that led to the Toronto Transit Commission implementing its Request Stop program. That meant, in the evenings, women could ask bus drivers to drop them off between stops, closer to their destination. And with this small extra step came a new and important message to the women of Toronto: "We will work harder to protect you because you deserve to be safe." Imagine if the alderman had just said that instead.

I remember as a kid, there'd be a story on the news about some old judge who decided to free an accused rapist because he decided the victim's clothing was too revealing. And then my mother would lose her shit. As a nurse and a psychiatric health care worker and a human being, she was disgusted by such backward thinking from someone in a position of authority. But how many people, especially kids, saw that news story and thought, *He's a judge. He knows best. Women who wear revealing clothing ARE asking for it.* Suddenly, the official discussion was not about a rapist's crime but what the victim did to deserve it.

No one deserves to be a victim of violent crime. And violent criminals don't deserve to have their actions rationalized away. We once heard from a victim's rights advocate after an episode where we talked being vigilant about personal safety. She pointed out that there are plenty of victims who were as vigilant as humanly possible and were attacked anyway.

She taught us that the sad truth is, you can't "stay out of the forest" because the world is a forest. And it's filled with predators. If someone is assaulted, it wasn't because they were careless, irresponsible, or dressed wrong. It happened because some piece of shit chose to assault them. And if someone is murdered, it's because some piece of shit chose to murder them. We need to turn the conversation toward identifying the behavior that leads to these attacks, figuring out how to identify these criminals faster and making sure their jail terms accurately reflect the seriousness of their crimes. And some of us need to unlearn the way we've been taught to think about the victims of those crimes. The following quote is from a TED Talk my sister sent to me that blew my mind:

We talk about how many women were raped last year, not about how many men raped women. We talk about how many girls in a school district were harassed last year, not about how many boys harassed girls. We talk about how many teenaged girls got pregnant in the state of Vermont last year, rather than how many men and teenaged boys got girls pregnant. So you can see how the use of this passive voice has a political effect. It shifts the focus off men and boys and onto girls and women. Even the term violence against women *is problematic. It's a passive construction. There's no active agent in the sentence. It's a bad thing that happens to women. It's a bad thing that happens to women, but when you look at that term* violence against women, *nobody is doing it to them. It just happens. Men aren't even a part of it!*

—JACKSON KATZ, PH.D., FROM HIS TED TALK "VIOLENCE AGAINST WOMEN: IT'S A MEN'S ISSUE"

Stay Out of the Forest: Final Thoughts

KAREN: What's the riskiest decision you've ever made, and how did it turn out?

GEORGIA: Quitting my desk job in 2009 (at almost thirty years old) to try to make it in the entertainment industry (specifically, hosting food shows). I'd lived my entire life paycheck to paycheck, so not having a regular salary or any guaranteed work was really scary, but I saw a chance and took it. My only goal was not to have to go back to a dreaded soul-sucking desk job, and so far, it's working! Giving myself the chance to try was pretty much the best, kindest decision I've ever made for myself.

KAREN: Have you ever intervened because you thought someone else might be in danger?

GEORGIA: I'm not at all shy when it comes to intervening. I've yelled at a woman for abusing her small child on a train, hugged a crying stranger in an airport, told a guy I overheard at a restaurant being a douche to his date that he was a douche, driven an old woman home when I saw her trip and fall on the sidewalk. To me, intervening is a much better way to be a human than being someone who minds their own business. Plus it gives you better stories to tell at parties.

KAREN: Tell us about the most interesting time you've ever interacted with the police.

GEORGIA: The time when we took an Uber to the airport in New Orleans after an *MFM* live show and the driver turned out to be a local cop. When he found out we gave away the glitter-covered shoe, given to us by the revered Krewe of Muses, to our Murderino bartender the night before, he lost his shit and almost kicked us out of the car. We had no idea how coveted and rare and precious those shoes are and that giving ours away was akin to saying we hated god. We're so sorry, Krewe of Muses.

art by Lauren Goldberg

FUCKIN' HOORAY!:
GEORGIA'S CONCLUSION

When I was about twenty years old, during the first gasp of the new millennium, I met a dude on a fledgling dating site called Makeoutclub. It was mostly hipsters with lip piercings (that'd be me) who wanted to meet other hipsters with lip piercings in their town. The guy I met and dated for a few months before we became lifelong friends (hi, Doug!) was one of those early internet people who knew about cool shit that you'd never heard of, like bands and local happenings, and would burn you copies of cassettes of super funny prank calls and made homemade video compilations of weird vintage commercials set to French pop music. Essentially, he was cooler than you but had endless enthusiasm about introducing people to said cool stuff, so he wasn't a douche. It was in that vein that he sat me down in the early stages of our dating life and put on his recorded-off-the-TV VHS copies of a low-fi cable show called *Mr. Show* that had already been canceled. I loved it and was in awe of what was happening on the TV, the hilarious, WTF sketches that always looped together by the end of the episode to form a crazy but dependable story arc. I'd never seen anything like it, but it felt like a familiar friend. Doug and I quoted it all the time and annoyed our friends by cracking each other up saying, "It's pumpkininny!" or "Stop needling me, you prick!"

When Doug found out that some of the comedians from *Mr. Show* regularly performed at a divey Italian restaurant on Fairfax Avenue called Largo, just a few minutes' drive from where I lived with my grandma, we immediately made plans to go. We were too broke to book a table at the restaurant, which would have guaranteed us a seat but also meant we had to order an expensive (for us) dinner to confirm our seating. Instead, we lurked around out front until the show was about to start, at which point the bouncer would or wouldn't let us come in and press up against the back wall, where we'd secretly sip cheap whiskey from a flask passed between us. There, in that tiny claustrophobic venue down the street from where my grandfathers had once run a butcher shop and barbershop, respectively, we saw fledgling comedians like Zach Galifianakis, Patton Oswalt, Sarah Silverman . . . and yes, even one Karen Kilgariff, perform to a spaghetti-eating crowd.

Karen was so funny—and confident, which, to a self-conscious twenty-year-old, also equals intimidating. Back then, there was no way I would have been able to speak to her with any sort of casualness. And she could have shot me down with one of her signature withering, caustic remarks had I tried, so I never did. But fifteen years later, after we had initially bonded over true crime at a Halloween party and I found out that we'd both be at Thanksgiving dinner at our mutual friend Joe's house, I was excited to have the chance to force her to be my friend. It's super fun when you get older and build confidence and know that you're good enough to be friends with anyone, no matter how big of a fan you are or how many times you saw them on TV. That even if they're a super funny, cool comedian that you've been in awe of for fifteen years, you're still good enough to be someone they think is cool, too. That takes a lot of time and self-care and LOTS OF THERAPY, but it is possible. I promise.

At Thanksgiving, which was just a small gathering of mostly awkward comedy dudes who didn't have the money to fly home to their families for both Thanksgiving *and* Christmas, I was totally myself, which meant loud belches so my cute but tight vintage dress would fit better and my inability to eat in silence (which you already know is my last lingering throwback to my eating disorder). So I asked a question to the assembled group, who were quietly masticating their stuffing and turkey while I tried not to gulp my whiskey on the rocks too fast, as I tend to do when I'm at an awkward social gathering.

"Hey!" I chirped. "Let's go around in a circle and each say something vulnerable!" I was in the middle of reading Brené Brown's *Daring Greatly,* which expounds upon the virtues of being an open book and essentially living your life with your heart on your sleeve in an effort to connect with the best parts of yourself and others. READ IT IMMEDIATELY, KIDS. *My Favorite Murder* wouldn't exist without it. Because despite Karen's confident exterior, it turns out she was withering in her own special brand of awkwardness, too that day, BUT she was also in the middle of reading *Daring Greatly,* which I found out when she perked up at her place on the sofa and asked if I'd read it.

The mostly awkward comedy dudes didn't share anything vulnerable about themselves that day, but Karen and I bonded immediately and shortly after made plans for lunch over Twitter Direct Message. That first lunch lasted for five hours, and in between stories about our lives, many of which you've just read, our conversation was peppered with our favorite murders. It was so fun and such a relief to start a friendship with someone from a place of vulnerability; I know that helped us connect right off the bat.

But also, when we came up with the idea for *My Favorite Murder* during the last month of 2015, we were both in pretty bad places in our lives, which isn't something we really talk about when asked about the podcast. We'll both vaguely reference how much it's changed our lives or how grateful we are for its success, which would be true even if we had both been living it up like Rihanna. But if you listen closely to those words, you'll hear a desperate gratefulness that surrounds them like an invisible cloud of the smoke that both our lives were in the midst of going up in.

My Favorite Murder saved my life in a lot of ways. I know that sounds dramatic, and of course I don't mean I was about to drive my car off the top of a parking-lot structure or anything, but at the time and for many years before, when I would lie awake at night and stare into the crystal ball that is anxiety, my future looked sad and bleak and stuck. While I loved so many aspects of my life, my wonderful, supportive relationship with Vince, our cute apartment and beloved cats, that I was healthy and didn't have to work a nine-to-five job, in other ways I was miserable.

My whole life was immersed in a career tied to a person with whom my relationship had become toxic. She and I didn't like each other anymore and resented that we had to continue to put on a façade of friendship in the name of money and increasingly distant potential success. Although, of course, I'd like to blame the whole thing on her, I'm working on living an examined life, so the reality is that we triggered each other, and the person I had become after being fully enmeshed in her life for seven years while we hustled to create a career together wasn't someone I'd want to be friends with either.

I was desperate for a way out, but my self-esteem had been so damaged by our toxic relationship that I felt like I was worthless without her, which I think she exacerbated due to her own issues. The confidence and tenacity I had when she and I had met, what had probably drawn her to want to be my friend in the first place, had been slowly scraped away. I felt broken, and I didn't know how to fix it, despite hours and hours of therapy.

I reached out to Karen to start a podcast out of desperation, really. I knew Karen was struggling, too, financially and creatively, so I threw a life raft to us, and we both gratefully grabbed on. Really, it was just a way for us both to have something *else*. Something creative and fun that didn't have the enormous stakes that every other endeavor in my life felt like it had. I had been trying SO HARD the prior few years to create something new, something I could be proud of and would make me feel like I had purpose.

My Favorite Murder was, from the very first episode, about vulnerability and a way to talk about a taboo subject that I wasn't ashamed to be interested in and that I felt was a legitimate topic that could benefit from being taken out of the "inappropriate to discuss in civil company" box so long as it was treated with the awareness and respect it deserved.

I was so excited to finally talk about this "weird" subject that I had been ob-fucking-sessed with since I was a kid with someone smart and funny and equally obsessed. It felt more like a therapy session than a podcast. In the months we had before it took off and became my main focus, everything else in my career went to shit. One night, after a long weekend working out of town for a food show the friend and I were on together, an exhausting job which after seven seasons of having to binge-eat desserts promised to give me diabetes and had started to rekindle my long-dormant eating disorder (having to eat fourteen doughnuts in two hours will do that to you). I was broken. I had nothing else to do to make money, but I just didn't care anymore. My soul was like, "Nope, you're done," and I knew I had to quit just to make room in my life to be happy enough to try something else. At least four years had gone by since I could reasonably say I was quitting while I was ahead. At this point, I was quitting before I was dead.

Shortly after, when *My Favorite Murder* hit number one on the iTunes comedy chart, I thought it was a mistake. Vince was the one who showed me, and I figured it just meant that we were number one on *his* chart's algorithms (hi, I'm not very computer savvy sometimes). When I showed it to Karen, she, in her infinite ability to downplay everything, told me not to get too excited. That it was indeed a fluke and I needed to chill the fuck out. But of course, in my infinite ability to daydream and scheme, I didn't chill the fuck out. We added mini episodes every week because I knew that the more episodes people have to listen to, the more listeners you'll get. We added new merch designs for sale based on the many quotes that listeners kept informing us were funny and important. We built this community of awesome (mostly) women who were just as ambitious and supportive and badass as we viewed ourselves to be, and who supported us even though we got names and dates and facts wrong and were very (*very*) far from perfect. I got to have the new life I wanted not despite of my imperfections but because my imperfections ended up being what was relatable and charming about me.

Thank fucking god I'm not a perfectionist, 'cause I really don't think any of those things would have happened had I needed everything to be just so. I think when you start out in life with low self-esteem and self-worth, your expectations for yourself are kinda lowered. That sounds super negative, but I actually am really stoked that for me, giving something your best shot is good enough, even if you fail. Aside from my grandma Mollie's favorite saying—"Bigger dummies than you"—I've also always had the question, "Why not me, too?" in the back of my mind. And while of course that *doesn't* apply to stuff like going to college and becoming a detective or going to culinary school, because as I've established, school and I don't mesh, it *does* apply to wanting to be a Cooking Channel personality or having a voice in true crime or having a top comedy podcast even though I'm not a comedian.

So it was in that spirit that I asked Karen if she wanted to start a true crime–comedy podcast. Why the hell not us, too?

The illusive Golden State Killer was caught this week, as I'm in the middle of writing this conclusion. After forty-plus years of not knowing the identity of the prolific rapist and murderer who terrorized

California in the '70s and '80s, DNA finally led law enforcement to the doorstep of an aging, unassuming grandfather who also happened to be a psychopath. Karen and I talked about this case over endless cups of black coffee at our very first hang-out lunch, and it was Karen's first murder that she did on the very first episode of the podcast. We praised Michelle McNamara, who had made this case her obsession and passion project, and had even given the fuckface murderer his new moniker, which without a doubt gave him more attractive branding and which caught people's attention so much better than EAR/ONS (East Area Rapist / Original Night Stalker). I was so insanely in awe of Michelle's tenacity and dogged determination. I wanted to be like her so much, instead of just a fangirl to rock stars like her and other journalists and the detectives who spent their lives chasing bad guys.

When Michelle unexpectedly died in April of 2016, halfway through writing her book about the Golden State Killer, I was so angry at the world. It felt so unfair. She was the good guy, and her death felt like the bad guy had claimed another win. When the killer was caught this week, one of my first thoughts was how freaking stoked Michelle would have been that he was finally going to answer for his crimes. I wanted to sit down with her for coffee and press the final pieces into the puzzle with her. I wanted to high-five her because even if law enforcement won't admit that she had a hand in tracking down this monster, we web sleuths (hey, Billy Jensen!) and the best detectives (hi, Paul Holes!) know the truth: if people like Michelle and other "armchair detectives" didn't give these cold cases attention, they would fade into obscurity.

Michelle's legacy will always be the Golden State Killer, and the period on that sentence is that, almost exactly a month after her book about the freezing-cold case was published, he was finally caught. That ain't no bullshit. Michelle galvanized the law enforcement community through her own rabid curiosity, a trait that I proudly share with her. (I finally did get to listen to the audiobook while cleaning out my closet, btw.)

My close friend Carey, a girl who collects crystals and is a fellow advocate of self-care through mental health, recently texted me a screengrab of a post from *My Favorite Murder*'s private chat room (she's kinda my spy in there) (I guess I just compromised her). A college student named Carley was in a class about feminism and social change and was working on a research paper about feminist movements. "So I am turning to my community to ask you how the rhetoric around *MFM* has changed your life and your idea of feminism?"

Under the screengrab, Carey texted, "If you're ever feeling down, just remember THIS. You led a feminist movement. That's a legacy that will live on without you!" I of course made a joke about how it sounded like she thought I was suicidal or she was preparing my eulogy, but if I had given vulnerability a shot in that moment, instead of the humor that I've relied on my whole life to shield me from intimate (read: awkward) moments, I would have just sent her a photo of myself crying, which is what actually occurred when I read her text.

Just two years ago, I could have never imagined that this would be my life . . . that I was someone who actually had a LEGACY to leave behind one day. Since MFM started, whenever I run into someone I know and haven't seen since the success of the podcast (which is A LOT in a city like LA), they always say something along the lines of "Can you believe it?!" or "Did you think this was going to happen??" or "How do you feel about all this craziness?!"

My answer is almost always the same: mouth slightly agape in speechless awe, a slow tremor-like shake of my head back and forth to portray my disbelief. Then I just mumble something about "It's crazy . . . I can't even . . . ," and I use my hands to mimic my head exploding. Then I change the subject. But what I really want to say is somewhere along the lines of "I am so fucking lucky. I am so fucking grateful. I think I deserve this, but I also can't believe it's happening. I promise to use my powers for good and not evil."

We've heard from so many people who have decided to go back to school to pursue a career related to true crime because of the podcast convincing them that their interest in murder is OK. These future criminal attorneys, police officers, forensic psychologists, and others have that empathy and goodness that is capable of changing the world.

The most important part of that legacy, one that Michelle was able to achieve through her terminal empathy and gorgeous poetic writing skills, is that in this world of true-crime obsession, it isn't about the blood, the gore, the terror, or the murderer. That shit is totally fascinating and we're all obsessed with it on some level, but at the end of the day, the only reason it matters is the victim. It's the victim and their friends and family who will forever be affected by the trueness of the crime long after the killer is caught or the popular tabloid case of the moment has moved on to something new.

I also feel incredibly grateful that Karen and I have listeners who help us learn from our mistakes and that we get to share those corrections on the podcast. I don't mean like how to pronounce awkwardly spelled city names in Wisconsin or whatever; I mean updating the language around crimes and violence in a way that acknowledges the victim's humanity. Like saying *sex worker* instead of *prostitute* and *died by* suicide instead of *committed.* And our listeners don't stop there. We're constantly blown away by the donations that Murderinos have made to important causes like End the Backlog and RAINN in our names and the friendships that have formed because the podcast brings together women with sharp minds and good hearts who are ready to be vulnerable and make a connection.

So when I say my standard polite acknowledgment of "I'm so lucky," what I really mean isn't that I'm lucky that the podcast got to the top of the iTunes charts or that we make enough money to cover rent or whatever; I mean that Karen and I are so lucky that we got a chance to show our vulnerable sides to each other without judgment, and through that, we created an imperfectly perfect legacy that is so much bigger than we are.

Stay Sexy. And Don't Get Murdered.

Elvis, want a cookie?

ACKNOWLEDGMENTS

KAREN

I'd like to thank my sister Laura Kilgariff, for her lifelong and continued older-sister excellence, as well as my other sister, Adrienne Kulasingam, for always being on my side. And I'd like to thank my father, Jim Kilgariff, for being the funniest person on the planet, the wisest man I've ever met, and the best father in the world.

GEORGIA

Thank you to my husband, Vince Averill. When my mind won't stop chasing anxious thoughts, you clothesline that fucker and wrap me in your hilarious chillness and for that I will always be grateful.

Thank you to my parents, Janet and Marty, for not disowning me when I was at my worst, and always being proud of me at my best, and everything in between.

Thanks to my siblings, Asher and Leah, for letting me share my childhood memories, which also belong to them, and not suing me for the stuff I get wrong. Thank you to my sister-in-law, Yolanda, for making our family seem slightly less neurotic. And to my two sweet, perfect nephews, Micah and Joe, for making me laugh and giving me hope for the future.

KAREN & GEORGIA

We want to thank everyone at Tor/Forge Books and Macmillan for their hard work and enthusiasm, Meredith Miller and the entire MFM Team at UTA, and STEVEN! Ray Morris for being there for us from the beginning.

We'd like to thank our brilliant editor, Ali Fisher, who truly made this book happen in every way.

ABOUT THE AUTHORS

Known for her biting wit and musical prowess, **Karen Kilgariff** has been a staple in the comedy world for decades. As a performer, she has appeared on *Mr. Show, The Book Group,* and *Conan.* She then transitioned to scripted television, writing for shows like *Other Space, Portlandia,* and *Baskets.* Her musical comedy album *Live at the Bootleg* was included in *Vulture's* 9 Best Stand-Up Specials and Albums of 2014.

Georgia Hardstark has enjoyed a successful career as a food writer and Cooking Channel on-camera personality, which began with the invention of the farcical cocktail the McNuggetini. She went on to cohost a travel/adventure/party show called *Tripping Out with Alie & Georgia,* and a regular gig on Cooking Channel's number-one show *Unique Sweets.* She capped that off as a repeat guest narrator on Comedy Central's hit show *Drunk History.*

For more information visit MyFavoriteMurder.com or follow My Favorite Murder:
Facebook: @MFMpodcast
Instagram: @myfavoritemurder
Twitter: @MyFavMurder

Visit Georgia Hardstark and her cats online:
Instagram: @hardstark and @elvisandmimianddot
Twitter: @GHardstark

Visit Karen Kilgariff on Twitter at @KarenKilgariff